Unpack Your Financial Baggage

How to Battle the Misconceptions of Retirement Planning

A Conversation with a CERTIFIED FINANCIAL PLANNER™ Professional

LOU MELONE, CFP®

Schuler Books
2660 28th Street SE
Grand Rapids, MI 49512
(616) 942-7330
www.schulerbooks.com

Unpack Your Financial Baggage: How to Battle the Misconceptions of Retirement Planning

ISBN 13: 9781948237772

Library of Congress Control Number: 2021905819

Printed in the United States by Chapbook Press.

"You cannot escape the responsibility of tomorrow by evading it today."

– Abraham Lincoln

Contents

About the Author

As a board CERTIFIED FINANCIAL PLANNER™ professional, Lou provides comprehensive financial planning strategies for higher net-worth families to help protect, preserve, and grow their current levels of wealth and plan for retirement.

With over 25 years of financial planning experience, Lou has focused on helping answer two critical questions, which most investors desire:

Do you know exactly how much money it is going to take for you to retire in comfort?

Do you know how much money it is going to take to remain comfortably retired?

Lou has championed a personalized and simplified approach to financial planning that is grounded in behavioral investing, with a strong commitment to a fiduciary standard of care.

Lou began his career with Dean Witter which merged into Morgan Stanley. He then moved his practice to Smith Barney, which merged into Citigroup. Decades ago, Lou recognized that many larger firms in the financial services industry were more focused on selling products than acting in the best interest of clients. As a result, he launched the registered investment advisory (RIA) firm Budd, Melone, & Company to provide comprehensive financial plans that are free from product conflict and put the client's interest first.

The final step for Lou was to launch Melone Private Wealth, which remains dedicated to meeting the fiduciary duty every day. Melone Private Wealth is a goal-focused, planning-driven firm aspiring to deliver the industry's premier client experience with carefully curated financial plans that are uniquely customized to each family's retirement goals, while using the most advanced technology.

This book is a continuation of Lou's dedication to teaching personal financial planning. Lou's simple and straightforward approach to explaining difficult financial industry concepts is part of his client-centric approach, which resonates with audiences that range from accountants to wealthy families to business owners to anyone who is struggling to understand the financial planning industry.

Lou has been recognized for his work and exceptional unending client care standard by being named a nine-time winner of the prestigious Five Star Wealth Manager Award as seen in *Forbes/ Fortune Magazine* and *Hour Detroit Magazine.*

Lou's unique perspective on financial planning has not gone unnoticed as he has been published or interviewed by *Thrive Global*, *Authority Magazine*, *Civic Center TV*, and *DBusiness Magazine's* RJ King for his "How to Grow Business" podcast. Additionally, he is a past columnist for *DBusiness Magazine*, Detroit's Premiere Business Journal. The accounting profession recognizes Lou's financial planning acumen as he is a past Contributor to the Michigan Association of Certified Public Accountants' (MICPA) knowledge hub, The Business Edge.

He has been a sought-after speaker for the MICPA since 2001 on topics that have ranged from Behavioral Finance, Comprehensive Financial Planning Process, and Types of Qualified Plans for Small Business Owners. In addition, Lou acts as a consultant for the MICPA Financial Planning Task Force.

The accounting profession is not alone in seeking Lou as a speaker and advisor as he presents planning/behavioral finance seminars to executive retiree groups at Fortune 500 companies, as well as other small to mid-size companies.

Introduction

Someone is sitting in the shade today because someone planted a tree a long time ago.

– Warren Buffett, chair Berkshire Hathaway

Tens of thousands of buffalo are stampeding through the open plains. The sun gleams down, trying to find its way through the immense dust cloud covering the landscape as this thunderous herd of loyal followers is led by the traditions and habits of a lead buffalo. The members of the herd are unaware of it, but they are racing towards the cliff to face a certain death.

Comparably, tens of millions of people are stampeding into retirement on their last major financial run expecting a retirement lifestyle of independence and dignity. Like the buffalo, they are following a leader off a financial cliff, due to the traditions and habits that have led to a misunderstanding of long-term planning—not to mention the prehistoric cognitive bias that is tugging at their behavior. In this case, the leader is not a person, but an archaic set of principles and practices hauled around in their minds by generations of misinformation and a culture that works against long-term planning. These ideas are packed into a mental suitcase that many people carry with them through retirement planning.

Your suitcase is full of these money habits and the traditions that come from our culture. You think to yourself, "How in the world did I get this much stuff in here? I don't remember even packing my suitcase, but it's full. I won't get to where I want to go with this much stuff, and it's too heavy of a burden to carry around." You pause one more time and reassess thinking, "This *can't* be mine." However, as you mentally check its contents, you realize, yeah, it's yours!

For up to sixty years you have been packing your suitcases – unconsciously – with inaccurate and unclear financial strategies and decisions. As you visualize your next thirty years, you have finally come to a realization that hits almost everyone at this point in life: it is time to repack my financial baggage to ensure our future; otherwise, my family and the generations thereafter will never get to where they want to go.

The best way to visualize this realization is through an initial conversation between a prospective client (or in this case the Suitcase Carrier) and a financial planner—a conversation which happens daily across America.

SC Carrier *We're looking to retire in the next few years, and we need to keep our money safe. You know, we don't want to lose it in the market.*

This is the mother of all misinformation. Although you may not see it yet—soon you will. With this simple two sentence statement, it is as if a hydra-headed beast of a misconception has jumped out of your suitcase with the focus on terms like *money, safe, and market.* But I digress, let us continue with the conversation.

Planner: *Let's say you've decided to fix your retirement income to an investment portfolio you've always thought of as being safe. You'll have to assume that your fixed income will always be enough to cover your living costs at today's prices and the next handful of years.*

In essence, you want to always have enough income to buy a three-dollar carton of milk. As the years pass, when that same milk costs $4, then $5, and then $6 a carton...and so on, what will you do then? At that point, how would you describe what's happening to your money? Does it feel, as you said, safe?

SC Carrier: *I'm not quite certain what you're trying to tell us.*

Planner: *I'm trying to reveal the issue of increasing living cost as an element of risk, in a potential three-decade retirement that the two of you will most likely experience, statistically speaking.*

SC Carrier: *Are you recommending we put everything in stocks rather than bonds? But at our age, don't you think the market is too risky and is going to crash soon?*

We have now uncovered the sister hydra-headed beast of delusion in the suitcase with phrases like *stocks are risky, at our age,* and *market crash.* The beasts are knocking the contents of the suitcase out onto the floor. Sorry, back to the conversation.

Planner: *Honestly, I'm not saying you should buy anything, and frankly, I'm not here to sell you anything. I don't know enough about both of you and your current financial situation to justify a recommendation, or to say if we're even a good fit for a planner/client relationship.*

All I'm suggesting is that you be open to a broader view of risk—one that accounts for decades of increasing living costs throughout your retirement. And by being open to this, it's the beginning of the wisdom of how planning and a financial planner can truly work for both of you.

SC Carrier: *Okay. But the economist on the news yesterday said there's going to be a recession coming. And the national debt in this country is out of control. Don't you think we should be concerned if that were to happen?*

Planner: *In regard to the economist's prediction—there's never a shortage of guessing on where the economy is going. Never. That's what economic forecasters are paid to do – make educated guesses. If I may quote the likes of Peter Lynch: "If you spend more than 13 minutes analyzing economic and market forecasts, you've wasted 10 minutes."*

However, if someone could identify exactly when a recession will begin—and end—we'd all sleep more soundly. Unfortunately, no one has ever done any of those things consistently—Ever.

And when it comes to the national level of debt, sure it's concerning. However, I don't know how anyone can craft a goal-focused, long-term financial plan, based on the income needs of a family (not to mention multiple generations) built on possibilities versus probabilities.

Over my twenty-five years in the planning industry, with history as a guide—the only guide we have—I have learned that anything is possible. However, two things absolutely ring true:

- **Successful investing is goal-focused and planning driven. In contrast, failed investing is market-focused and event-driven.**

- **Successful investors act constantly on their plans. Conversely, failed investors react continually to the markets.**

Pause for a moment and read those last two points above again. Did you read them? Now, again. The wisdom of financial planning and the key to unpacking your misconceptions in the suitcase are wrapped up in these two simple but powerful statements.

You see, this entire conversation (*or verbal dance*) we have been witnessing, whether you are aware of it or not, has been rooted in two deep-seated unknowable uncertainties. First, the initial questions posed by all clients/prospective clients is nothing more or less than unconsciously asking permission to unload the suitcase, which means permission to stop carrying around the long-held worries that their history, conditioning, and the media have been telling them that they need to worry about.

And second, the concerns about current events, markets, economics, pandemics (or whatever) are never really *the issue*. The issue is an unasked question from them to the planner: *Can we believe and trust you with our life savings which we've worked so hard to earn?*

Planning is a disciplined process of navigating rationality while enduring the uncertainties of life's challenges. In addition, successful investing and planning is countercultural because as humans we are enmeshed in a culture that:

- prioritizes spending over saving
- urges us to seek big returns fast rather than focus on long-term strategies
- gives us a misguided notion of what is safe in terms of money and investments.

In other words, our instincts are hard-wired with beliefs that are destructive to our family's financial well-being. Working with a financial planner to secure a comfortable retirement involves overcoming what we learn from our culture, often through the media.

Now, breathe.

This book will enable you to accomplish the simple, everyday, common sense principles and practices of financial planning to acquire long-term wealth for both the family and those you cherish most. It's all delivered by the confessions of and conversations with a certified financial planning professional with over twenty-five years of stewarding the ship of financial independence for higher net-worth families.

I assure you that it will be a painless process that will not delve into some esoteric or theoretical concepts. Nor will you need a PhD in mathematics. And *you will not hear these on any newscast/ social media outlet.* Why? Quite frankly, they are just too damn boring. However, *boring is the way* to build, grow and preserve long-term wealth that your family and potentially multi-generations of your family cannot outlive. These tried-and-true simple secrets will benefit all those who choose to follow—and this leader's advice will not run you over the cliff.

Let's pause here and ask a basic question.

Why is a generation inundated with more education on how to plan and invest for retirement than any in history still riddled with misconceptions that will lead to their financial doom?

Could it be what the famous money manager, Peter Lynch, once wrote? "You cannot get a high school diploma in this country without once having known what a cosine is. However, you'd go home with that same diploma on graduation day—never having been taught the difference between a stock and a bond." Maybe. Although I believe today's twenty-four-hour news cycle is really the primary cause.

How, you may ask, do I know that the primary cause of the problem isn't lack of education, as it may have been at one point, but is now something else? One word. DALBAR. We will spend an entire chapter on what has been revealed over the past thirty years by the DALBAR study of Quantitative Analysis of Investor Behavior (QAIB). Yeah—that is a mouthful, but in short, the study provides the actual returns of the average equity fund investor compared to the performance of the stock market—measured by the Standard and Poor's 500 (S&P 500) index. *It reveals that the average investor not only underperformed the overall market but their own investments.* Yes, I know it sounds strange. But true.

Let me further explain. In an article from *The Wall Street Journal* on December 31, 2009, Eleanor Laise reported the best performing mutual fund of the decade. You see, the fund that Laise was describing was the $3.7 billion CGM Focus Fund and according to *The Wall Street Journal*, which used Morningstar research, it had an astonishing return of 18% per year for the last decade, ending December 29, 2009.

Any investor that was an owner of equities over that decade surely will attest that this thing knocked the cover off the ball. And I know what you're thinking, since we tend to have a rear-view mirror approach to most things in life: I MISSED IT. Now, before you pick up the phone to have a conversation with your financial advisor, it seems as if even those who owned the fund missed out.

According to Morningstar, the average shareholder of the fund during the same decade had a *loss of 11% per year*. Wait—how was it that the fund returned 18% and the average investor in the same fund lost 11%, the fund's dollar-weighted return? A quick refresher, 18% is the fund's time-weighted return, which is for a specific period (what the manager did). On the other hand, the dollar-weighted rate of return (-11%) is the actual returns that average investors received, based on either adding or pulling monies out.

When asked about the gap between his returns verses the average shareholder, the fund manager, Kenneth Heebner said: "A huge amount of money came in right when the performance was at a peak...we don't have any control over what investors do." To be more precise, just after the fund surged 80% in 2007, investors poured in $2.6 billion at the peak. Soon afterward, it plunged 48% and as a result, by November of 2009, investors had pulled out $750 million.

How could this happen? As the chart below (Domestic Equity Funds vs. Net New Flows) from Davis Advisors reveals, if you track the net money flow (line) of all Domestic Equity funds since 1997, you can see that investors have historically poured money in right after the market peaks (shown as the bars) and then sell as the market pulls back.

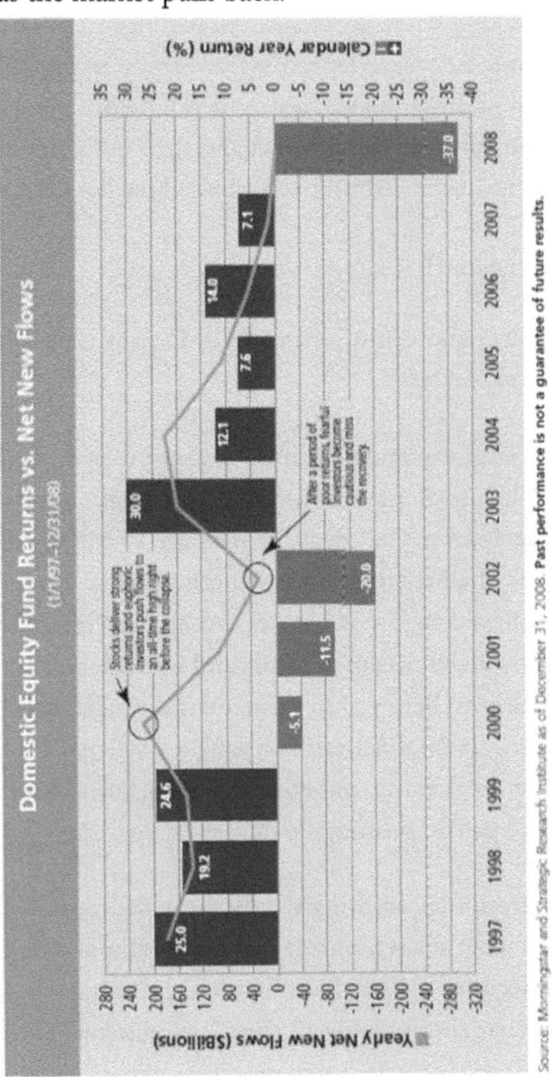

To recap, let's take a walk down Rearview Mirror Lane; 1) as the market/fund just came off an incredible year, more money was added at a higher price; 2) when the markets were in turmoil, money was pulled out at the low; and 3) the manic-depressive cycle of buying high and selling low continued.

Furthermore, after a few decades of the findings from DALBAR, the CEO wrote a cover letter to the 2014 study saying: "Despite all the left-brain information and advice that have become limitlessly available to investors in this internet age, their behavior has not changed." Conclusion: investor education alone does not work.

Then, I say again, why?

As the famous radio commentator, Paul Harvey used to say, "*And now, the rest of the story.*"

What is the largest population in retirement today? The baby boomers. Who are children of whom? Those who were growing up immediately after the Great Depression. What *mindset* do you think they had about planning and investing? Not a good one. They believed the stock market caused the Great Depression (*which it did not*), banks are not safe, and individuals can rely on the government to help you in retirement through social security (*yes, this is an oversimplification, but you get my point).* In summary: do not invest, work until you retire at age 65, and collect Social Security until you're "pushing up daisies" at age 72.

As a result, from their upbringing, the baby boomers relied primarily on what for retirement income? Company Pensions and Social Security. What about financial planning advice? Non-existent. In turn, they would call their "stockbroker" for investments "tips" and they confused this with what *they thought* was financial planning. Which is as far from it as you can possibly get, but I digress.

At the end of the day, it may come as somewhat of a surprise to know that the elite planners, those who are worth multiples of what they charge, have one thing in common—they do not manage money. They manage people. Essentially, saving those families' most cherished lifelong goals and dreams from the enemy—Human Nature.

Human nature is defined by Lord Edwin E. Hitti as "a bundle of characteristics including ways of thinking, feeling, and acting which humans are said to have naturally...the essence of humanity." For purposes of financial planning, we are not concerned with the philosophical component. Instead, we'll focus on the physical and physiological aspects, which lead us to want to do things because "I've done that before." Or in plain English, stated by Warren Buffett's teacher, Benjamin Graham; "The investor's chief problem—and even worst enemy—is likely to be himself."

If you did not quite grasp the above concept, let me be a bit more—let's say—blunt. **Human nature is a failed investor** (*sorry to be the messenger of reality*). We cannot escape the normal, natural emotions and behaviors which have been hard-wired into all of us since the Neanderthals were running from saber-toothed tigers. However, with some guidance you will be able to recognize all the hydra-headed killing behaviors as they continually present themselves throughout your family's multigenerational wealth planning.

Some of those behaviors we will address are:

- Loss Aversion
- Mental Accounting
- Anchoring
- Regret
- Herding

Now a question: Do you know what successful planning and investing looks like? I am not talking about listening to the waterfall of untreated financial media sewage about planning and investing. If you are truly honest you will have to admit you probably do not know how to recognize successful planning, let alone how to construct it.

What is my proof? In part, the 30th Annual Retirement Confidence Survey (RCS) conducted by the Employee Benefit Research Institute (EBRI) and independent research firm Greenwald & Associates.

The RCS is the longest-running survey of its kind, measuring worker and retiree confidence about retirement. The 2020 survey of 2,042 Americans was conducted with an online research panel between January 6 and 21, 2020. All respondents were ages 25 or older. The main survey included 1,018 workers and 1,024 retirees.

My own name for this study is "American Perception versus Reality." From a behavioral finance viewpoint, it highlights overconfidence bias.

Here are the key findings:

Figures of current workers found that 7 out of 10 workers (69%) are confident in having enough money for a comfortable retirement (Worker Attitudes Towards Retirement Preparations). This is great news to read, though it specifically focuses on what I have called *perceptions.* In spite of this perception of preparedness, 61% say that preparing for retirement makes them stressed out. This is an understandable by-product.

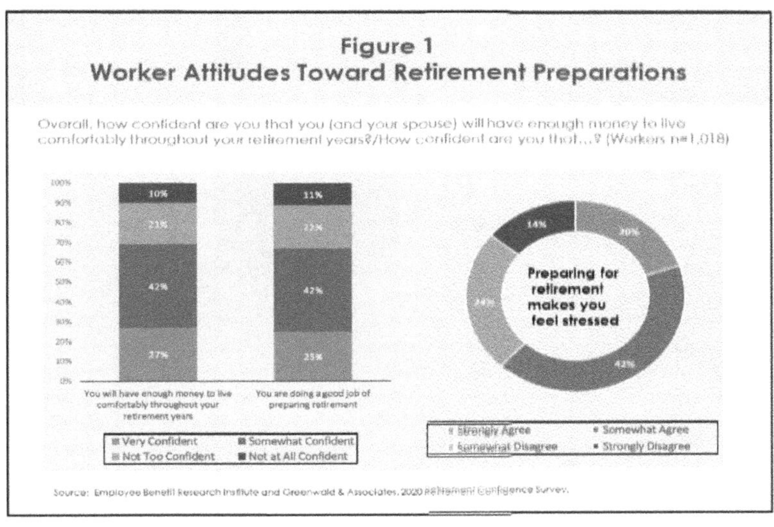

Source: Employee Benefit Research Institute and Greenwald & Associates, 2020 Retirement Confidence Survey.

However, ***only 48% of all workers have calculated how much they will need in retirement*** (Percentage of Workers Calculating Retirement Needs). Yes. You read this correctly—go ahead, read it one more time and take it in. Are you part of this forty-eight percent? Furthermore, fewer than four in ten have planned for emergency expenses, how much they will need to withdraw from savings monthly, or how much is needed to cover health expenses. I call this *reality.*

Figure 4
Percentage of Workers Calculating Retirement Needs

Have you (or your spouse) tried to figure out how much money you will need to have saved by the time you retire so that you can live comfortably in retirement?
Workers n=896*, Percent Yes

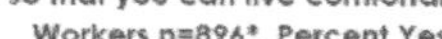

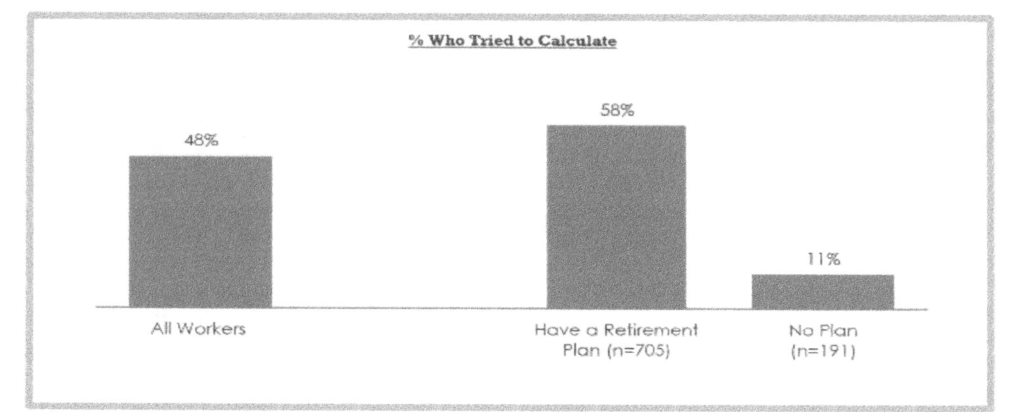

Have Retirement Plan defined as respondent or spouse having at least one of the following: IRA, DC plan, or DB plan.

Source: Employee Benefit Research Institute and Greenwald & Associates, 2020 Retirement Confidence Survey.
Figures and n sizes presented exclude those who answered "Don't know", said they never worked, or refused to answer.

But wait, there are more confusing responses; the four in ten workers who tried to calculate what they need for retirement estimate they will need $1 million or more. However, only 30% of all workers have saved over $250,000 or more for retirement (Workers Savings Amounts, by Plan vs. No Plan).

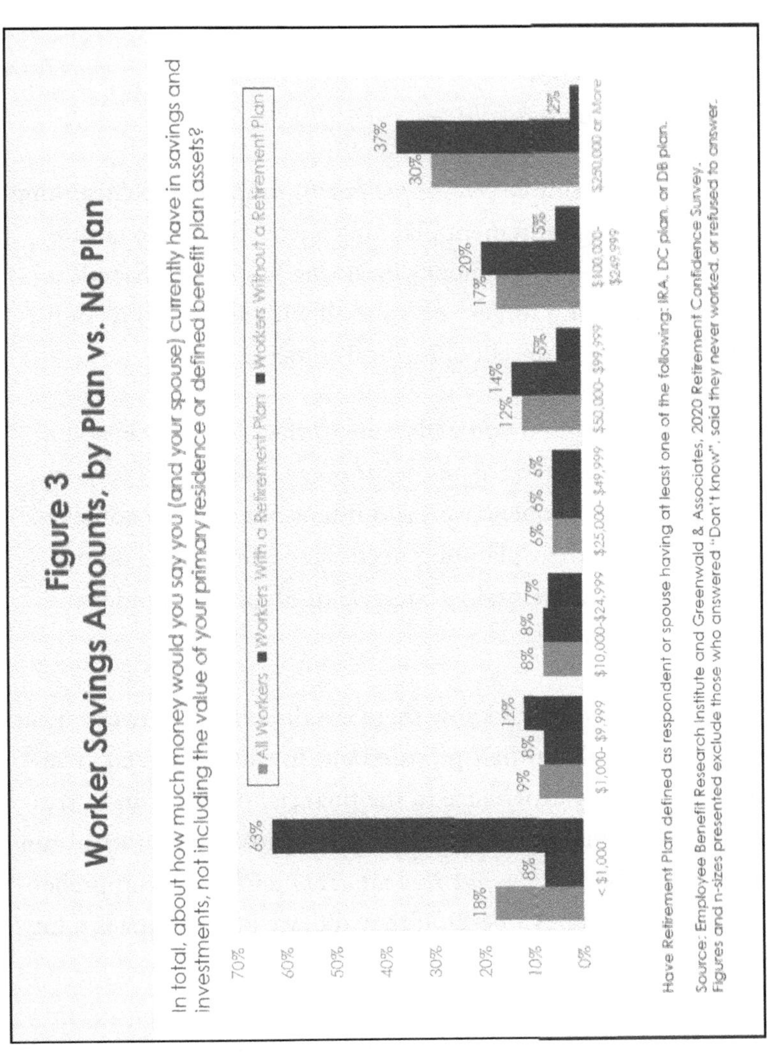

Whether they believe they have a financial plan or not, workers are most likely to get the retirement planning resources they need from the following sources (in order of prevalence):

1) Family and Friends
2) Employer/Work
3) Google/Online Search
4) Financial Advisor
5) Online Calculators

Can we make a simple (*maybe not exact*) comparison that seeking critical, life-long retirement planning advice needed to ensure you accumulate enough money by asking family and friends is akin to performing surgery on yourself with advice from Aunt Betsy's aspiring high school medical student?

Think about this and you will come to the same conclusion as I have—*what is perceived and what is done can be worlds apart.* Although most people have good intentions when it comes to retirement and their planning needs, good intentions do not pay the bills and maintain a lifestyle of dignity and independence in retirement.

The other reason why I know there is a disconnect between what people believe about their preparedness for retirement and reality? Based on my experience in the financial planning industry, working with higher-net worth families across the country, I can tell you that few had (*before they sat down with me*) a comprehensive financial plan. And even if they did, we had to unpack a lot of useless and outdated items.

Once asked about a plan, they would say something to the effect of, "Oh, yeah, I got one of those things (*title of printed-off five-*

page generic template of nothingness) that my person at (*insert Wall Street Firm*) gave me." (This was most likely done just before the stockbroker threw some Morningstar asset allocation report in front of them to show how *their* funds can outperform the "other advisor." Which they can't guarantee…but let's not allow facts to cloud the stockbroker's sales pitch). There I go giving you my industry bias. Back to the conversation.

My response was usually, "Have you updated your income and expenses yearly, based on your family's long-term goals? Long-term goals reflect your cash flow needs in retirement—for the lifestyle-sustaining income both of you require. Also, have you linked that cash flow need to a diversified portfolio which will continue to rise, as the cost of living will surely do? Oh, and finally, have you updated or reviewed with your Estate Planning Attorney the documents to pass on your family's wealth to the next generation in the most tax efficient way permissible by law?"

SC Carrier: *(Crickets…silence). Yeah, yah-know, we meant to do that but…*

Planner: *Understood. The fact that the amount of money saved by the average couple in America is earmarked for retirement leads inevitably to these two facts which must be faced honestly (ego aside), as it's the only way to reach the land of financial freedom:*

1) Either the money outlives the person, or
2) The person outlives the money.

The only determinate of said outcomes will be accomplished (or not) by the existence or non-existence of a comprehensive financial plan.

SC Carrier: *I haven't thought about it that way, but that seems clear now.*

Planner: *Knowing these facts, the questions posed to both of you are these:*

1) Do you know exactly how much money it's going to take for you to be able to retire comfortably—and to remain comfortably retired?

2) Would you be open to me helping you figure it out—understanding that there'll be no cost to you in my doing so?

Alphabet Soup of Credentials and Advice

If you can't convince them, confuse them.

– Harry S. Truman, U.S. President 1945–1953

Chauffeur Knowledge.

At the 2007 Commencement to the USC Law School, Charlie Munger, business partner to Warren Buffett of Berkshire Hathaway, explained what he called chauffeur knowledge this way:

> I frequently tell the apocryphal story about how Max Planck, after he won the Nobel Prize, went around Germany giving the same standard lecture on the new quantum mechanics.
>
> Over time, his chauffeur memorized the lecture and said, "Would you mind, Professor Planck, because it's so boring to stay in our routine. [What if] I gave the lecture in Munich and you just sat in front wearing my chauffeur's hat?" Planck said, "Why not?"
>
> And the chauffeur got up and gave this long lecture on quantum mechanics. After which a physics professor stood up and asked a perfectly ghastly question. The real chauffeur, unable to answer, said, "Well, I'm surprised that in an advanced city like Munich I get such an elementary question. I'm going to ask my chauffeur to reply."

Munger continues:

> In this world we have two kinds of knowledge. One is Planck knowledge, the people who really know. They've paid the dues; they have the aptitude. And then we've got chauffeur knowledge. They've learned the talk. They may have a big head of hair, they may have fine timbre in the voice, they'll make a hell of an impression.
>
> But in the end, all they have is chauffeur knowledge. I think I've just described practically every politician in the United States.
>
> And you are going to have the problem in your life of getting the responsibility into the people with the Planck knowledge and away from the people with the chauffeur knowledge.

Before we go any further, it is imperative you understand who is providing the planning advice you are receiving and if said advice is what Mr. Munger calls, chauffeur knowledge. Have you ever been confused as to what your advisor's credentials are, how they were achieved, or what type of criteria were used to get the "alphabet soup" you find in the financial industry?

Our industry does a terrible job of helping the public understand the difference amongst each firm or people's primary function. Most families do not realize that most internally driven titles are awarded by how much commission that person generated in the year. For example, vice-president of investment or senior vice president are both based on commission.

In addition, titles like Retirement Planning Specialist are awarded by taking a computer-based test (given by that firm) which takes about an hour to complete, and voila you are an expert in the public's eyes. There are only a handful of credentials that are overseen by a non-biased, independent board that require continuing education and each has a specific advice category for its designation.

According to the Certified Financial Planner Board of Standards website, the list of designations below includes some recognized by the industry which are achieved through independent sources requiring continuing education and ongoing ethical standards. In addition, to apply for the final examination, some level of either college or graduate coursework must have been completed. (*For those professionals in our industry that are reading this, yes, I know there are a few more titles that are independent, but these are the dominant identifiers*).

CERTIFIED FINANCIAL PLANNER™ (CFP®):

> Certificants are individuals who have met CFP Board's education, examination, and experience requirements; have agreed to abide by the CFP® Board's Code of Ethics and Professional Responsibility; and who complete CFP Board's biennial certification requirements, including continuing education, to use the certification marks. Certificants have passed a one day six-hour exam.

Chartered Financial Consultant (ChFC):

> Generally used by financial professionals—including accountants, attorneys, bankers, insurance agents and

brokers, and securities representatives—who have earned the ChFC designation by completing The American College's eight-course education program, met experience requirements, and agreed to uphold a code of ethics.

Chartered Financial Analyst® (CFA®):

Holders of this designation are generally securities analysts, money managers, and investment advisers who have completed the CFA program, a graduate-level, self-study curriculum and examination program for investment professionals that covers a broad range of investment topics. CFA charter-holders are required to affirm their commitment to high ethical standards.

Certified Investment Management Analyst℠ (CIMA®):

Offered through the Investment Management Consultants Association, the CIMA certification program is a credential designed specifically for financial professionals who want to attain a level of competency as an advanced investment consultant. The CIMA professional integrates a complex body of investment knowledge to provide objective investment advice and guidance to individuals and institutions. The CIMA certification program requires that candidates meet all eligibility requirements, including experience, education, examination, and ethics.

Now, if your current advisor does not hold any of the aforementioned independently offered titles, it does not mean that he or she is incompetent in the services they are providing you.

However, as an investor you should ask the person who you have trusted your family's long-term financial well-being, "What requirements were needed to achieve the current designation or title you are flashing on your card or media site?" Again, you want to know if it was independently offered or internally provided through their own firm, where, as mentioned many times, a title is awarded based on production (commission) alone.

Unfortunately, the lack of understanding regarding who awards designations and titles, as well as the requirements for receiving them, is what has led to the public's confusion as to what services and competence they are going to be provided when they initially meet with their financial person. You should question any title or designation to find out how it was received and what it really means.

To put an end to this confusion, my suggestion would be that the clarification needs to be more in line with other professional advice givers. For example, in the accounting industry you are either an accountant or have achieved your CPA designation. If you are an attorney, you have passed the bar examination and are now a J.D. With these other industries, which make up a person's financial team, it is simple and clear cut. No Alphabet Soup.

Another area our industry adds confusion to the public is with respect to what it means to be a fiduciary. Should the public be concerned if their person is not held to the standard of fiduciary?

There are 6 core fiduciary duties, according to the Institute for The Fiduciary Standard:

1. Serve the client's best interest
2. Act in utmost good faith

3. Act prudently—with the care, skill, and judgment of a professional
4. Avoid conflicts of interest
5. Disclose all material facts
6. Control investment expenses

A higher level of oversight traditionally has come from those who hold themselves out as fiduciaries to their clients. Unfortunately, the Securities and Exchange Commission (SEC), having recently implemented a "Best Interest" (BI) regulation, just added to the smoke and mirrors of the industry.

Ron Rhoades, a fiduciary law expert, is interviewed in June of 2019 for *ThinkAdvisor Magazine* as saying that the Securities and Exchange Commission has committed "the greatest securities fraud in history" by adopting Regulation Best Interest, making Broker-Dealers (BDs) "pretend fiduciaries" who think their duty of care can be satisfied by disclosing conflicts of interest, a belief that's "ludicrous." In other words, the Best Interest is not enough to ensure that the advisor will adhere to all six of the duties outlined by The Fiduciary Standard.

In plain English, what does all this mean to the average investor?

In the bigger picture, all advisors fall into one of three categories:

1. Broker
2. Independent Advisor
3. Duel Registered Advisor

Let us break down each area:

Broker: The majority of advisors in this country, over ninety percent, are brokers. Again, put aside the alphabet soup of titles they flash to you on their card. They are brokers, which means they are paid a fee or commission for selling you a financial product.

Where are they employed? Wall Street firms, brokerage houses, insurance companies. What standard are they held to when providing advice? It used to be called a "Suitability Standard," but now it is the new regulations mentioned earlier of "Best Interest." Good or Bad? Let us just say that the bar is not set high.

Independent Advisor: Of the roughly over three hundred thousand advisors in the country, only about 10% are independent advisors. They are also called Registered Investment Advisors (RIA). RIA's usually charge a flat fee for providing advice or a percentage of the clients' assets under their management. No commission.

They are normally smaller, non-Wall Street, independent planning, and investment firms. What standard are they held to when providing advice? The highest level, called a Fiduciary Duty, and they must disclose any conflicts of interest in writing in their ADV. An ADV is a form submitted by investment advisors to register with both the SEC and state securities authorities. It is essentially a disclosure document on the operations of the advisor.

Duel Registered Advisor: Simply, the advisor can be registered as either of the above options. Mainly independent advisory firms register as duel and not the larger brokerage houses. The distinction to understand here is to know when they are acting as a broker (selling product) or providing advice as an RIA.

The Plan

If you don't know where you're going, you might not get there.

– Yogi Berra, baseball catcher, manager, and coach

Two older gentlemen are sitting in a park, chatting about their investment portfolios. The discussion:

Gentleman 1: *I've outperformed the market* ***by 3% a year.*** *Pretty impressive, yes?*

Gentleman 2: *That's great, I only matched the market's returns. That must be why I ran out of money five years ago when I was 75.*

Gentleman 1: *That's too bad. Hey, I'm 80 years old, also...*

Gentleman 2: *(mumbles) You must be doing pretty well by outperforming the markets by 3% per year?*

Gentleman 1: *I, ah, ran out of money at 79.*

Most Americans will look at this everyday occurrence and say something like, "Sounds about right to me. I've heard this discussion many times, and frankly I've been in that conversation about performance." What is missing from this conversation, which happens countless times throughout our country? They haven't calculated the income they need, at the average rate of growth or sustainable withdrawal rate, in order to live comfortably throughout retirement.

Unfortunately, many retirees come to this realization too late in life to save themselves from the agony of trying to survive on Social Security alone. They believed that the *goal* was all about investment returns and outperformance.

You see, the average investor's misconception mixes with what they do not know. And by not knowing what they do not know, they are focused on the tail and not the dog. In this case, the tail is the portfolio (investments), and the dog is the plan. *Never allow the tail to wag the dog.*

Here is a reality check: Investment outperformance, is *NOT* a financial goal. Having an income you cannot outlive, instead of the other way around—this is a financial goal. Accumulating enough money to retire on comfortably—this is a financial goal.

These goals lead to the next important questions:

1. What is financial planning?
2. Why should anyone want to plan (*warning, this gets boring*)?

Let us break it down. First, what is financial planning?

In the broadest sense, financial planning is the process of making decisions about your long-term financial goals and managing your income, expenses, debt, and investments in order to meet those goals. For the purposes of this book, we are more specifically focused on financial planning to meet your retirement goals.

Financial planning can feel as uncertain as predicting the weather on a certain day twenty years from now. Although it is confusing for much of the investing public—perpetrated by our industry's allowed use of subjective titles for professionals (*as mentioned earlier)*—there is only one independent governing board for financial planning, The Certified Financial Planner Board of Standards, Inc. (CFP Board).

The CFP Board is a non-profit organization that serves the public by fostering professional standards in personal financial planning. They set and enforce the requirements for CERTIFIED FINANCIAL PLANNER™ certification "to create competent and ethical financial planners who are committed to putting their clients' best interests first" (*their words, not mine, from their site).*

The Certified Financial Planning Board Code of Ethics and Standards of Conduct lists seven practice standards for the financial planning process, and all Certified Financial Planners (CFP®) must adhere to these standards as fiduciaries (*more on the importance of a fiduciary later*).

A CFP® Professional must adhere to the Code of Ethics in several ways:

1. Act with honesty, integrity, competence, and diligence
2. Act in the client's best interest
3. Exercise due care
4. Avoid or disclose and manage conflicts of interest
5. Maintain the confidentiality and protect the privacy of client information
6. Act in a manner that reflects positively on the financial planning profession and CFP® certification

The CFP® Practice Standards require knowledge and action on the part of the financial planner, including the following:

1. Understanding the client's personal and financial circumstances
2. Identifying and selecting goals
3. Analyzing the client's current course of action and potential alternative courses of action
4. Developing financial planning recommendations
5. Presenting the financial planning recommendations
6. Implementing the financial planning recommendations
7. Monitoring progress and updating

Not to pile on any further, but do you see a requirement for outperforming the market anywhere in those standards? No. Why? There is NO historical evidence for the persistence of performance. None. So, planning is *the way* to financial independence—hence the process for reaching goals, but it is not a guarantee of outcome. Can we now move on from this point because I am beginning to lose interest myself?

Simply stated: Financial planning for retirement requires saving for the future, essentially an act of delayed gratification to set aside today's dollars to achieve a stated goal for you, your family, and future generations. That's it. Not a difficult concept to grasp, but it can be a tremendously difficult task to accomplish in our world of instant gratification where our prehistoric cognitive bias directs us to accumulate. A world where the media and the marketing divisions of companies are telling you to live for today. Daily—no, every second of the day—we are walking around as the media (*driven by its marketers*) is tugging at our emotional wants. The constant marketing hides a deeper truth. Most of us do not *need* a new phone, computer, or furniture *today*. We may want it, but most likely it is not a *need* to get accomplished today. If put off until the near future, it does not become a detriment to your life.

Why should we plan? As Richard Cushing says, *"Always plan ahead, it wasn't raining when Noah built the Ark."*

Financial planning isn't another purchase that can be delayed. It is a need that must be accomplished or begun today. Why? Because you cannot get today back and every minute your money is left to the *silent killers of time and neglect*, you become a statistic of the big misconception at the beginning of our planner/prospective client discussion, focusing on the wrong issues: "Money." "Safe."

Which leads us to the next question, what is money? Better yet, if you reach into your pocket and pull out a green piece of paper with a dead president on it—what would you call this? Go ahead. Say it. Yes, most Americans would say *MONEY*. And they would be exactly wrong.

The simplest way to explain this is by continuing our prior conversation:

SC Carrier: *Again, we want to keep our money safe.*

Planner: *For my own understanding, as we all have different definitions of words—how would both of you define safe?*

SC Carrier: *Well, I guess the safest thing our fathers once told us was to keep it locked up in the house. That's a bit extreme but yah know the old saying about the safest place being under the mattress. That means nobody can steal it or use it up. The same amount will always be there.*

Planner: *OK. So, let's say the million dollars was placed under a mattress. And twenty years later you both walk over to that same bed, lift the mattress, and see the million dollars. Would you both say that you've preserved your money, or in your words, kept it safe?*

SC Carrier: *Well, yeah. It's still there isn't it? But why do I feel like you're going to tell us differently?*

Planner: *It's nice to hear you're both becoming open minded about how planning really works. Let me show you something that will pull it all together. What do you see here?*

1965 Postage Stamp
5 Cents

2020 Postage Stamp
55 Cents

SC Carrier: *I got this one…postage stamps.*

Planner: *Exactly. And the one on the left is a U.S. postage stamp from 1965 that costs five cents, while the one on the right from 2020 costs fifty-five cents.*

SC Carrier: *We're with you.*

Planner: *Great. The one on the left is from when you both were born and the one on the right is from today. Let's say that the 1965 stamps represent everything you need to live on each year up to retirement. Meaning all your expenses of home, utilities, food, travel, insurance, taxes, entertainment—basically your standard of living.*

SC Carrier: *Yep, we get it. Our lifestyle we are accustomed to.*

Planner: *Yes. Now, as costs rise, to get as much as you previously bought with a five-cent stamp, you now need something else. Any guess as to what that is?*

SC Carrier: *The fifty-five-cent stamp. So, everything is costing us more, right?*

Planner: *Yes. Where did you get the money to pay for that additional cost? You had to walk over to the mattress, correct?*

When you were both born, every dollar under that mattress was chewed up by the five-cent cost of living and you felt comfortable or safe.

Fast forward to us sitting here today and that same five cents would now have to be fifty-five cents to accomplish the same thing. In essence, you've walked over to your mattress each year and every dollar you pick up is now smaller. It's like tearing each dollar in pieces.

How "safe" are you feeling about that money now, under the mattress?

SC Carrier: *When you put it that way, we don't really like that much. We're feeling much less safe about our parents' advice.*

Planner: *All this discussion is showing you that MONEY (as you believed from your upbringing) is not defined as units of currency, which the masses of people walking around today also believe.*

Simply stated, today's dead president is not the same, or at least worth the same, as next year's dead president. The magician's (let's call it inflation) sleight of hand under the mattress, just took that dollar over the years and made it less, much less.

All this being said, would you both agree that the more realistic definition of money is purchasing power?

This concept reminds me of something Warren Buffett once explained to his 2011 shareholders in his annual report. *I have taken this explanation below in its entirety for two simple reasons: 1) I cannot summarize it any better, and 2) it is just that important to all investors to comprehend these planning and investing concepts.*

The Basic Choices for Investors and the One We Strongly Prefer (The Full 2011 Letter to Shareholders can be viewed at www.berkshirehathaway.com)

Investing is often described as the process of laying out money now in the expectation of receiving more money in the future. At Berkshire we take a more demanding approach, defining investing as the transfer to others of purchasing power now with the reasoned expectation of receiving more purchasing power—*after taxes have been paid on nominal gains*—in the future. More succinctly, investing is forgoing consumption now in order to have the ability to consume more at a later date.

From our definition there flows an important corollary: The riskiness of an investment is *not* measured by beta (a Wall Street term encompassing volatility and often used in measuring risk) but rather by the probability—the *reasoned* probability—of that investment causing its owner a loss of purchasing power over his contemplated holding period. Assets can fluctuate greatly in price and not be risky, as long as they are reasonably certain to deliver increased purchasing power over their holding period. And as we will see, a non-fluctuating asset can be laden with risk.

Investment possibilities are both many and varied. There are three major categories, however, and it's important to understand the characteristics of each. So, let's survey the field.

Investments that are denominated in a given currency include money-market funds, bonds, mortgages, bank deposits, and other instruments. Most of these currency-based investments are thought of as "safe." In truth they are among the most dangerous of assets. Their beta may be zero, but their risk is huge.

Over the past century these instruments have destroyed the purchasing power of investors in many countries, even as the holders continued to receive timely payments of interest and principal. This ugly result, moreover, will forever recur. Governments determine the ultimate value of money, and systemic forces will sometimes cause them to gravitate to policies that produce inflation. From time to time such policies spin out of control.

Even in the U.S., where the wish for a stable currency is strong, the dollar has fallen a staggering 86% in value since 1965, when I took over management of Berkshire. It takes no less than $7 today to buy what $1 did at that time. Consequently, a tax-free institution would have needed 4.3% interest annually from bond investments over that period to simply maintain its purchasing power. Its managers would have been kidding themselves if they thought of *any* portion of that interest as "income."

For tax-paying investors like you and me, the picture has been far worse. During the same 47-year period, continuous rolling of U.S. Treasury bills produced 5.7% annually. That sounds satisfactory. But if an individual investor paid personal income taxes at a rate averaging 25%, this 5.7% return would have yielded *nothing* in the way of real income. This investor's visible income tax would have stripped him of 1.4 points of the stated yield, and the invisible inflation tax would have devoured the remaining 4.3 points. It's noteworthy that the implicit inflation "tax" was more than triple the explicit income tax that our investor probably thought of as his main burden. "In God We Trust" may be imprinted on our currency, but the hand that activates our government's printing press has been all too human.

High interest rates, of course, can compensate purchasers for the inflation risk they face with currency-based investments—and indeed, rates in the early 1980s did that job nicely. Current rates, however, do not come close to offsetting the purchasing-power risk that investors assume. Right now, bonds should come with a warning label.

Beyond the requirements that liquidity and regulators impose on us, we will purchase currency-related securities only if they offer the possibility of unusual gain—either because a particular credit is mispriced, as can occur in periodic junk-bond debacles, or because rates rise to a level that offers the possibility of realizing substantial capital gains on high-grade bonds when rates fall. Though we've exploited both opportunities in the past—and may do so again—we are now 180 degrees removed from such prospects. Today, a wry comment that Wall Streeter Shelby Cullom Davis made long ago seems apt: "Bonds promoted as offering risk-free returns are now priced to deliver return-free risk."

The second major category of investments involves assets that will never produce anything, but that are purchased in the buyer's hope that someone else—who also knows that the assets will be forever unproductive—will pay more for them in the future. Tulips, of all things, briefly became a favorite of such buyers in the 17th century.

This type of investment requires an expanding pool of buyers, who, in turn, are enticed because they believe the buying pool will expand still further. Owners are *not* inspired by what the asset itself can produce—it will remain lifeless forever—but rather by the belief that others will desire it even more avidly in the future.

The major asset in this category is gold, currently a huge favorite of investors who fear almost all other assets, especially paper money (of whose value, as noted, they are right to be fearful). Gold, however, has two significant shortcomings, being neither of much use nor procreative. True, gold has some industrial and decorative utility, but the demand for these purposes is both limited and incapable of soaking up new production. Meanwhile, if you own one ounce of gold for an eternity, you will still own one ounce at its end.

What motivates most gold purchasers is their belief that the ranks of the fearful will grow. During the past decade that belief has proved correct. Beyond that, the rising price has on its own generated additional buying enthusiasm, attracting purchasers who see the rise as validating an investment thesis. As "bandwagon" investors join any party, they create their own truth—*for a while.*

Over the past 15 years, both Internet stocks and houses have demonstrated the extraordinary excesses that can be created by combining an initially sensible thesis with well-publicized rising prices. In these bubbles, an army of originally skeptical investors succumbed to the "proof" delivered by the market, and the pool of buyers—for a time—expanded sufficiently to keep the bandwagon rolling. But bubbles blown large enough inevitably pop. And then the old proverb is confirmed once again: "What the wise man does in the beginning, the fool does in the end."

Today the world's gold stock is about 170,000 metric tons. If all of this gold were melded together, it would form a cube of about 68 feet per side. (Picture it fitting comfortably within a baseball infield.) At $1,750 per ounce —gold's price as I write this—its value would be $9.6 trillion. Call this cube pile A.

Let's now create a pile B costing an equal amount. For that, we could buy *all* U.S. cropland (400 million acres with output of about $200 billion annually), plus 16 Exxon Mobils (the world's most profitable company, one earning more than $40 billion annually). After these purchases, we would have about $1 trillion left over for walking-around money (no sense feeling strapped after this buying binge). Can you imagine an investor with $9.6 trillion selecting pile A over pile B?

Beyond the staggering valuation given the existing stock of gold, current prices make today's annual production of gold command about $160 billion. Buyers—whether jewelry and industrial users, frightened individuals, or speculators—must continually absorb this additional supply to merely maintain an equilibrium at present prices.

A century from now the 400 million acres of farmland will have produced staggering amounts of corn, wheat, cotton, and other crops—and will continue to produce that valuable bounty, whatever the currency may be. Exxon Mobil will probably have delivered trillions of dollars in dividends to its owners and will also hold assets worth many more trillions (and remember, you get 16 Exxon Mobils). The 170,000 tons of gold will be unchanged in size and still incapable of producing anything. You can fondle the cube, but it will not respond.

Admittedly, when people a century from now are fearful, it's likely many will still rush to gold. I'm confident, however, that the $9.6 trillion current valuation of pile A will compound over the century at a rate far inferior to that achieved by pile B.

Our first two categories enjoy maximum popularity at peaks of fear: Terror over economic collapse drives individuals to currency-based assets, most particularly U.S. obligations, and fear of currency collapse fosters movement to sterile assets such as gold. We heard "cash is king" in late 2008, just when cash should have been deployed rather than held. Similarly, we heard "cash is trash" in the early 1980s just when fixed-dollar investments were at their most attractive level in memory. On those occasions, investors who required a supportive crowd paid dearly for that comfort.

My own preference—and you knew this was coming—is our third category: investment in productive assets, whether businesses, farms, or real estate. Ideally, these assets should have the ability in inflationary times to deliver output that will retain its purchasing-power value while requiring a minimum of new capital investment. Farms, real estate, and many businesses such as Coca-Cola, IBM and our own See's Candy meet that double-barreled test. Certain other companies—think of our regulated utilities, for example—fail it because inflation places heavy capital requirements on them. To earn more, their owners must invest more. Even so, these investments will remain superior to nonproductive or currency-based assets.

Whether the currency a century from now is based on gold, seashells, shark teeth, or a piece of paper (as today), people will be willing to exchange a couple of minutes of their daily labor for a Coca-Cola or some See's peanut brittle. In the future the U.S. population will move more goods, consume more food, and require more living space than it does now. People will forever exchange what they produce for what others produce.

Our country's businesses will continue to efficiently deliver goods and services wanted by our citizens. Metaphorically, these commercial "cows" will live for centuries and give ever greater quantities of "milk" to boot. Their value will be determined not by the medium of exchange but rather by their capacity to deliver milk. Proceeds from the sale of the milk will compound for the owners of the cows, just as they did during the 20th century when the Dow increased from 66 to 11,497 (and paid loads of dividends as well). Berkshire's goal will be to increase its ownership of first-class businesses. Our

> first choice will be to own them in their entirety—but we will also be owners by way of holding sizable amounts of marketable stocks. I believe that over any extended period of time this category of investing will prove to be the runaway winner among the three we've examined. More important, it will be *by far* the safest.

Now back to the conversation:

SC Carrier: *OK. Understood. So, if I'm doing the math correctly, over a 30-year period $1 is the same as $2.43 at 3% Inflation.*

Planner: *Yes. Knowing now the silent killer we call inflation will attack you and your family for the next thirty years of retirement, as you sit here today and look over the remainder of your life, retirement boils down to one primary question that must be addressed:*

Are you highly confident that your retirement income will be enough to sustain your lifestyle, or are you at all concerned at some point you may run out of money?

SC Carrier: *We were confident before we began this discussion, but now knowing the mattress was not the best advice, not so much.*

Planner: *You're not alone. This is where most couples in your phase of life are. That's what the plan is for: having a goal-focused, date-and-dollar-specific roadmap to help your income continue to rise as the cost of living continues to rise. The goal is to have our income outlast us rather than us outlast our income. Agreed?*

SC Carrier: *Agreed. Does it make sense to plan for the possibility of a lower inflation rate or does it seem possible that inflation will go up soon? How can we plan for this?*

We have now come to the point in the conversation when a new reality is beginning to set in. This is both good and bad. Why? We have just sliced off two heads of the beast (money and purchasing power), but it has not begun to turn tail and run away. The suitcase just let loose another misconception—Possibility versus Probability.

Planner: *Are you a fan of comedies?*

SC Carrier: *Sure, we both like a good laugh. Hopefully, it's not at our expense.*

Planner: *Not at all. There is a scene from the movie, Dumb and Dumber, which reveals a simple intelligence in the foolishness of Lloyd (played by Jim Carey). It goes like this:*

Lloyd: I want to ask you a question, straight out, flat out, and I want you to give me the honest answer. What do you think the chances are of a guy like me and a girl like you ending up together?

Mary: Well Lloyd, that's difficult to say. We really don't…

Lloyd: Hit me with it! Just give it to me straight! I came a long way just to see you Mary, just… The least you can do is level with me. What are my chances?

Mary: Not good.

Lloyd: You mean, not good like one out of a hundred?

Mary: I'd say more like one out of a million.

Lloyd: So, you're telling me there's a chance. YEAH!

SC Carrier: *Love that movie...didn't really relate it to planning, but we get it.*

Although the media is awash with feeding every American family the possibilities, we in the real world of financial planning can only plan with probabilities. Why? All else is prognostication or what is called "soothsaying." And the fatal mistake families transitioning into retirement make is *reacting* to the current possibilities of market events or a crisis—and by doing so they have now redefined what they believed was a plan.

Just to drive the proverbial stake into the beast one last time, theoretically speaking, anything is possible (I've been around long enough to never say never) but if everyone acted on these theories, most people would fear getting out of bed in the morning.

For example, let's say you live in a state where you must step into your car to drive to work. What is preventing the oncoming car from crossing that narrow yellow line painted between both of you? Is it some magical paint? No. Is it possible they will cross? Yes. But in all *probability*, they will not. So, instead of dealing with the possibility of them hitting you, you drive confidently and arrive at your planned destination. Just like the financial plan.

Now that doesn't say that over time, you weren't delayed getting into work due to some sort of temporary issue (snowstorm, rainstorm, accident, road construction, or other issue), but you made small adjustments in your drive to get to your destination. In the same fashion, your plan is a living breathing document that will need to be adjusted as "life happens" with a birth, death, job change, disability, or other life events. This is called annually updating your plan. The key word here is *annually*. You might be surprised to see that there is no mention of making adjustments for market or economic events throughout the year. That's because we are focusing on long-term planning.

At this point, you may be asking the question, "How do we know what the dollar amount is for us to retire comfortably, and what is the process (in comprehensive financial planning) that will help us solve those issues of how to provide a comfortable retirement income we can't outlive?"

Glad you asked (or I asked for you).

Let us revisit the golden two (2) questions asked in the opening of the book. Go ahead and re-read them, I'll wait here.

> ***1. Do you know exactly how much money it's going to take for you to be able to retire comfortably—and to remain comfortably retired?***
>
> ***2. Would you be open to me helping you figure it out—understanding that there'll be no cost to you in my doing so?***

Now, let's continue the conversation in the first meeting.

Planner: *Imagine that you're not retiring in ten years but at the end of this month. Make believe that next month is your first full month in retirement. Now, over and above social security and any pension benefits you may have in retirement, about how much money do you think you'd need to withdraw from your retirement savings, before taxes, in order to sustain your lifestyle next month?*

SC Carrier: *Um, we haven't really thought about it that way, but I guess we could come up with a rough figure. … [Silence, thinking]. Since neither of us will be getting a pension…Let's say…um, about $15,000—no, around $10,000 a month. Yeah, that should be enough.*

Planner: *Ok, so you will need $120,000 in your first year of retirement.*

What has just happened? The couple had to place a real figure on living expenses (*maybe the first time ever*). The reason the question was asked for a monthly figure is quite simple: in my experience, this is the most difficult number to get from someone in the planning process. Honestly, it isn't uncommon for it to take a few years into the relationship (*if they become a client*) to obtain the exact figure for our plan. It's much easier for people to imagine a monthly figure, and, if I were to have asked for a yearly figure, I would have gotten blank stares.

Planner: *But you're not retiring at the end of this month; you're planning on retiring in ten years. Therefore, we'll simply inflate that figure you gave me by three percent—which is the trendline inflation or the silent killer—for ten years.*

What it reveals is—assuming this is the lifestyle you both would like to continue in retirement—the dollar amounts you'll be needing to withdraw from your investments. Are you both following my line of thought?

SC Carrier: *Yes. We are onboard.*

Planner: *Good. So, $120,000 today is the same as $160,00 in ten years (using a round number for ease of conversation).*

SC Carrier: *Hold on. Say that again.*

Planner: *Remember our conversation regarding the postage stamps? This is the reality of those stamps in today's conversation.*

SC Carrier: *Oh, yeah. Money under the mattress and purchasing power. Yep.*

Planner: *Now, the amount of capital (pile of money) you will need in ten years to begin withdrawing from in order to provide both of you that monthly income is $3,600,000.*

SC Carrier: *Seriously? (with eyes wide open, jaw to the table) How did you get this figure?*

Planner: *Using historical market returns over the longest of timeframes, which we will cover later, and a comfortable withdraw rate from that pile of money of about 4.5% per year. This will allow for the portfolio we design for you to provide you with the income you require and NOT to deplete your principal.*

In plain English, you both live the lifestyle you deserve, and the value of the portfolio continues to rise to leave a legacy to those you cherish most.

Now, my recommendation is for both of you to go home and think about the figure you gave me—making any adjustments you feel are needed. When you've done that, we can have a follow up meeting—if you'd like—and craft a specific plan to get you from where you are today to that retirement figure. This is what we do at our firm. That is planning.

SC Carrier: *But what if I don't plan on living until at 90, will we need that much money?*

Planner: *Fair enough. When do you plan on dying? You have a specific date?*

SC Carrier: *Well, no, but our family history doesn't last that long. Maybe age 75.*

Planner: *So, what'll happen if we plan for your "family date" of death and it doesn't happen?*

SC Carrier: *Well, um…I'm not sure, just wanted to see if that will reduce the amount of money we have to save?*

Planner: *I see. (5 second pause) Is it at all important to you that your spouse and children continue to grow and preserve your family's legacy?*

SC Carrier: *Absolutely. Very Important.*

Planner: *(silently looking at the couple).*

SC Carrier: *Ok, I get it. We can move on.*

If we have not scared off the retiring couple (bodies curled up in shock at a home bunker), during the second meeting we will delve into the figures provided between meetings and present the recommendations to the prospective clients. This will encompass the following:

- Current Financial Position (where you are today, how assets are titled, amount of debt)
- Financial Priorities and Goals
- Net Worth (assets minus liabilities)
- Cash Flow Planning (income and expenses)
- Savings and Contributions (how much, if any, is left over each year plus contributions to retirement plans, college education)
- Asset Allocation (how your portfolio is currently invested)
- Protection (life, disability, and long-term care insurance amounts)

Once all these areas are input to both the planner and prospective client's comfort, we will enter a Decision Center in our interactive planning software. It will provide, in real-time, the answers to the golden question: How long will my money last? Visually, we can see if the money goes into the abyss or continues for future generations. Depending on the outcome, we can make real-time adjustments for multiple possible scenarios while in the meeting.

The sample case below shows (in dark grey) the current scenario of the prospective client before any recommendations. They ran out of money at age 87 (where the bar goes into the abyss or reaches zero on the chart). The light grey bars (layered above) show how long the money will last after we make some live planning decisions. You will see that by making some lifestyle adjustments with assets (selling of vacation home), retirement ages (delayed retirement by 3 years), and the expenses to support their elderly parents, the portfolio gains around 1.6 Million over their lifetime and lasts until age 95.

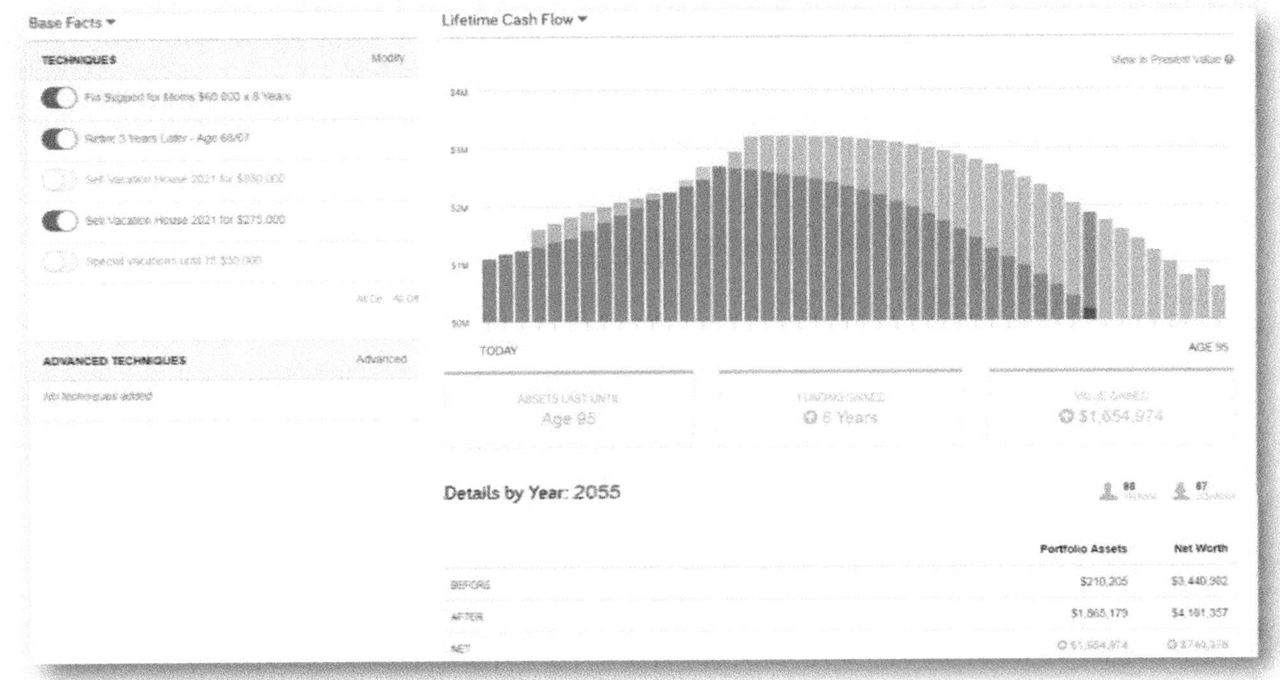

Base Facts
TECHNIQUES
Modify
Sell Vacation House 2021 for $275,000
ADVANCED TECHNIQUES
Advanced
Lifetime Cash Flow
$4M
$3M
$2M
$1M
$0M
TODAY
AGE 95
Age 95
6 Years
$1,654,974
Details by Year: 2055
Portfolio Assets
Net Worth
BEFORE
$210,205
$3,440,982
AFTER
$1,865,179
$4,181,357
NET

Once the cashflow issues are solved, we begin analyzing using the Distribution Center in our interactive estate planning. Here, we can make decisions on how the family's legacy will continue to future generations and allow for charitable giving in the most tax efficient structure.

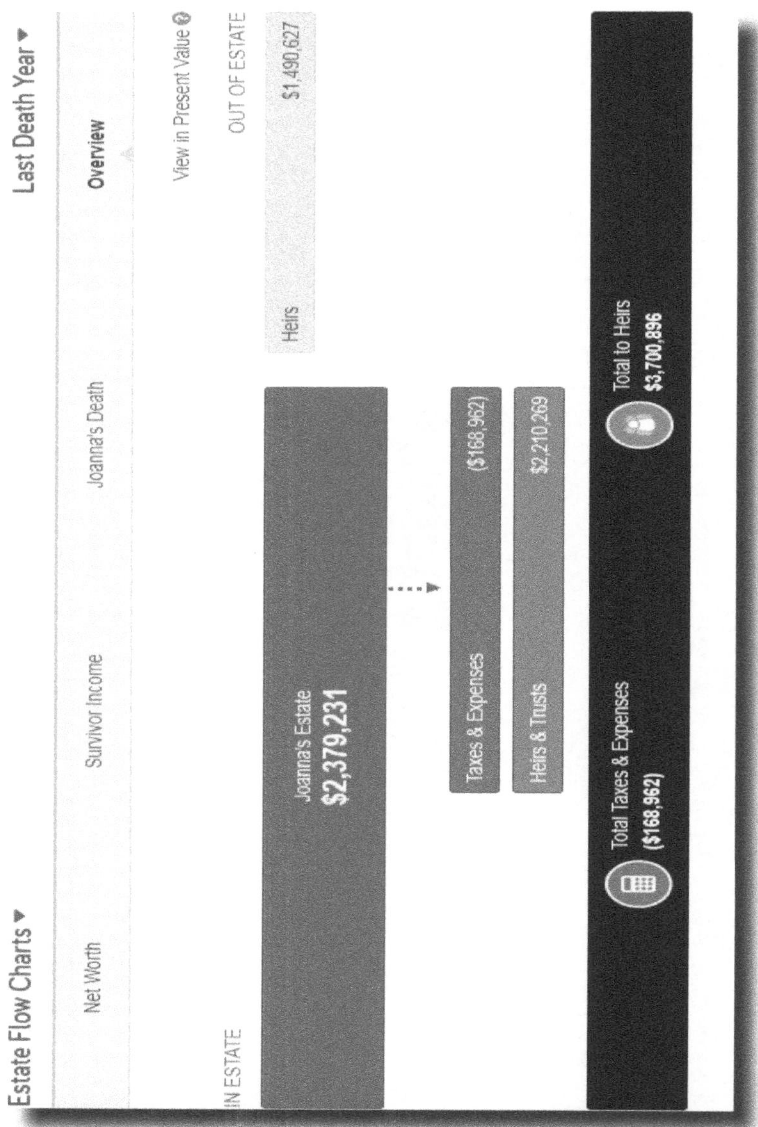

Let's return to the conversation.

SC Carrier: *Ok, since we're going to need that amount of money to retire, what type of returns have you gotten your clients that we can expect?*

Planner: *Returns?*

SC Carrier: *Yes, I mean your performance for the clients like us?*

Planner: *I have about 120 clients. Which is about the number of families with investment portfolios uniquely designed to fund the needs of their comprehensive plan we've crafted. In that sense, I'd be challenged to tell you the exact "return."*

SC Carrier: *I think you lost us there.*

Planner: *As I've mentioned during this conversation, I'm a financial planner first and my clients' portfolios are the funding mechanism for their lifetime plan. A portfolio is simply a tool for the realization of my clients' goals; it's never an end in itself.*

As a refresher, the first thing we'll determine is what you're trying to accomplish, the timeframe you've got to accomplish it, and the resources to achieve your goals. Then, we develop an investment strategy, a plan for reaching your goals. Finally, I design a portfolio using long-term historical returns, to get you where you need to go.

Now the hard part. Once we've created a beautifully diversified portfolio of investments that are suited to your comprehensive plan and cash flow needs, I become your behavioral coach. Coaching you, over the next thirty years to make good financial decisions and avoid making emotional decisions regarding the portfolio.

My approach is goal-focused and planning-driven, rather than being based on some attempt to outguess the economy or the markets. I'm convinced that successful investing involves constantly ***acting*** *toward your goals, and unsuccessful investing is based on* ***reacting*** *to whatever the markets are doing at the moment or abandoning the plan for immediate gratification.*

Does the planning approach we've gone over make sense to both of you as a way for us to begin? Or do either of you have any questions?

SC Carrier: *No question at this point.*

Planner: *As I have mentioned, my philosophy is that the dominant factor determining the long-term investment returns people get in real life is their own behavior. As an example, the issue won't be in predicting when markets will peak or bottom out—which no one can do, if they are truthful—but guiding how clients respond to those phases of euphoria at market peaks, and to the potential panic, both of which are normal human reactions at market bottoms.*

In addition, I would never have tried to prognosticate when the dot.com bubble would have ended in the year 1999 or 2000. Our discussions would have been in trying to make sure clients never got exposed to dot.com mania to begin with. On the other hand, I won't be guessing when a declining market will bottom (as you've listened to ad-nauseum on the cable news sites). Instead, my conversations will be geared toward guiding clients not to panic out of a bear market, but to continue to invest at end-of-world prices, which would enable them to get much closer to their goals we'd laid out in our plan.

By providing your family with this behavioral advice, I can't guarantee that your investments will be outperforming the market at any given moment, however, I'm fairly confident in saying that you'd be achieving better long-term results than most, primarily because I'd helped you avoid the most common human mistakes that investors are making just about every day.

Quite frankly, much of the behavioral coaching you'll both be receiving is a value that is intangible. In other words, it's not something that will show up on your monthly statement in the short run, as most would like to see. However, it will provide an enormous amount of "anxiety free" lifetime planning, as you'll be witness to as the wealth begins to compound over multiple generations of your family. This is true wealth.

Now, I've given you an enormous amount to think about, and I appreciate both of you giving me the time to explain what we do (our process of planning) and how I believe we provide value to our clients.

Chapter Takeaways:

- Investment outperformance is NOT a financial goal. Having an income you cannot outlive, instead of the other way around—this is a financial goal. Accumulating enough money to retire on comfortably—this is a financial goal.

- A financial plan or financial planning is essentially an act of delayed gratification, meaning, setting aside today's dollars to achieve a stated goal for you, your family, or multiple generations of family in the future.

- MONEY is not defined as units of currency, which the masses of people walking around today believe. Money is purchasing power.

- The silent killer of retirement is inflation, as represented by the postage stamps.

The Principles and Practices

The pleasure which we are to enjoy ten years hence interests us so little in comparison with that which we may enjoy today.

– *Adam Smith,* The Theory of Moral Sentiments, *1759*

What do the elite planners focus their time and attention towards in attempting to control the critical variables that will most likely dictate the success of their clients' families' most cherished long-term, real-life goals?

The Three Principles: Mindset, Patience, and Discipline.

These three principles are imperative to the success of investors' lifetime achievement to true multigenerational wealth. Why? They represent the belief system that directs decision making. And as we are all aware, what you think dictates what you do. Said another way, belief leads to actions.

The first principle, *Mindset*, is your beliefs about or attitude toward the future. Which are you? Optimist, pessimist, or realist. Many are pessimists, for example, best described by a character from *Saturday Night Live*, Debbie Downer. Debbie Downer was a fictional character introduced in 2004. The character's name, which refers to someone who frequently brings bad news or negative feelings to a discussion, brings down the mood of everyone in any conversation she engages in. We all know someone just like this. In the planning world, we would refer to this character's trait as a pessimist or (*to the extreme*) a catastrophist.

In all the years I've been coaching the behavior of client families, the mindset is the dominant driver of their success as an investor. Nothing else that follows remotely holds a close second. If a person wakes up every day in constant fear that at any moment the-world-as-they-know-it is on the brink of collapse (*world events, politics, interest rates, war, or the business cycle...blah, blah, blah*) no matter how impeccable their plan or investments have been crafted to their unique lifelong dreams and desires—*they will blow it up.* The ever-pulling fear, reinforced by the media's need to manifest a crisis, will be too strong to resist.

However, do not confuse this disease with a normal, healthy dose of realism or questioning the conventional wisdom. All investors should question why the specific process of planning was recommended for them and their families. Because this mindset will require some element of a belief in the future, as investing is an act of placing todays' money away to utilize at some point in the future, and the future is unknowable, it's wise to consider probable outcomes and plan accordingly.

This leads back to my prior statement of rationality during uncertainty. And it is that exact uncertainty which draws out the fears and behaviors which have continued to plague all investors. As Warren Buffett says, "*Temperament is more important than IQ,*" in successful investing.

The second principle that will deliver a high probability to the investors long-term success is *Patience.* Yes, we have all heard the saying, patience is a virtue. However, when it pertains to lifelong planning and investing, it is a necessity. Why? Our current culture of social media and 24/7 news cycles with the talking heads pontificating what will happen now, the urge to do "something" can be overwhelmingly challenging. This is why I call my planning and investment strategy *countercultural*—it goes against the prevailing norms of our culture. In addition, you must have the patience to resist our current social media culture, which has been coded to not only influence your decisions but to anticipate (through Artificial Intelligence Algorithms) and guide your next decision—all beneath your consciousness. You may be saying, no way, that's conspiracy thinking. Not according to the Netflix documentary *Social Dilemma* by Jeff Orlowski.

The documentary interviews multiple programmers, coders and software engineers who originally designed the platforms for Google, Facebook, Twitter, Instagram and more. They explain that the manipulation of human behavior has been "coded in" to these companies for profit. Social media sites make money because they are designed to keep users paralyzed (*my words*) and engaged so they don't leave their sites, which enables the advertisers to try and sell you something. And that something is specifically determined by algorithms that use your habits to predict and promote future purchases. These algorithms work, as proven by the billions of dollars of revenues between them. It takes patience and determination to delay gratification so you can achieve your goals.

Another way you need patience is to resist investment advice that encourages you to react to short-term changes in the market, often promoted by the media, especially on investment shows. If you question this or just want to test your resolve, go ahead and tune into CNBC for just a few minutes. I have tested my personal resolve in the past and even with all my understanding and study of how the mind works (cognitive bias and emotional pulls), after a small segment designed to keep people watching by providing provoking news and investment strategies, I have found my thoughts poking at my subconscious saying, *Maybe I should be doing something*. Yes, I am human just as you are. As a side note, if you want to know who their true audience is, pay close attention to the advertisers on the following shows: *Mad Money*, *Fast Money*, *Squawk Box* (a reference to the old days of stockbrokers), *American Greed*, *Closing Bell*, and *Power Lunch*. I. Rest. My. Case.

It's easy to see why clients who watch these shows might lose patience. My response over the years to clients (*once engulfed by the emotion*) has always been, "If your goals haven't changed, don't change your plan and if your plan hasn't changed, don't change the portfolio. Allow the planning process to work."

You may be wondering, what happens to those who give into the destructive behavior and lose their patience? Here are a few examples:

In the book, *Thinking, Fast and Slow* by Daniel Kahneman, who won the Nobel Memorial Prize in Economic Sciences, he reveals a few studies by Terry Odean and Brad Barber. The first, performed by Terry Odean, a professor of finance at UC Berkley, studied the trading records of over 10,000 brokerage accounts of individual investors over a seven-year period.

In this time, he was able to analyze over 163,000 trades. In doing so, he tracked both what the investor (*I would accurately define as speculator*) sold and what was purchased to provide a comparison of the returns of each action, over the next year. The results were—how would you say, ah—not good. On average, the shares that the traders sold did better than those that they bought by a margin of over 3.2% per year.

In later research, Terry Odean and colleague Brad Barber wrote a paper entitled, "Trading is Hazardous to your Wealth." It revealed that, on average, the most active traders had the poorest results. And the investors who traded the least had the best results.

What does all this research tell us? The siren song of the financial media—fueled by a need to generate "eyeball revenue or clickbait"—is tugging on your brain's weakness to Just. Do. Something (*financially speaking*). For such times as these, we can find a calming truth from a hidden treasure of our childhood past. ***"Doing nothing often leads to the very best of something."* —*Winnie the Pooh***

The third and final principle is *Discipline*. The act of not *reacting* and instead doing what has always worked. Let me explain this practice from an article I wrote back in January of 2011 for *Dbusiness Magazine*. It was titled, "Modern Day Rip Van Winkle."

> Most individuals are aware of the story of Rip Van Winkle, the young Dutch American in the story published in June of 1819 by author Washington Irving. As a refresher, it's a story of a young farm owner who was not the most ambitious individual. However, he was quick to lend a hand to any neighbor who may have needed help or to do whatever would get him away from tending his daily chores on the farm.
>
> Well, one day as he is procrastinating (*my interpretation*) he follows a guy into the mountain that is carrying a keg; he drinks a few and falls asleep…for twenty years. Upon waking, with hair and beard long and grey, he returns to the village to find nobody he recognizes, and he's

unaware of the changes that have taken place over time. You may be thinking, nice story but how does this relate to investments and financial planning? Well, what would you have missed if you fell asleep on March 11th, 2008 and woke up January 7th, 2011? Not twenty years later, but a little over two years.

To review this time period, let us look back and use my favorite source for crisis material, the financial media. The reason for your sleep on the above date is because the Federal Reserve had just outlined a two hundred-billion-dollar loan package to bail out the banks and upon hearing this news you figured it would be a good day to have a drink. While you are dreaming, the following has happened:

- *March 16th, 2008*: The Federal Reserve approves a $30-billion-dollar loan for JP Morgan to take over Bear Stearns.
- *December 19th, 2008*: President Bush outlines loans for GM and Chrysler for $17.4 billion to survive the next four (4) months.
- *February* 17th, 2009: Stimulus Bill for $787 billion
- *March 6th, 2009:* Unemployment hits 8.1 percent
- *March 12th, 2009:* Madoff Ponzi Scheme hits the news
- *April 30th, 2009:* Chrysler files for bankruptcy
- *June 2009:* General Motors files for bankruptcy

SNOORE, SNOORE, SNOORE (*Yes, you are still sleeping*).

- *April 2010*: Greece Debt Crisis
- *May 6th, 2010:* Flash Crash, Dow drops around 600 points in about fifteen minutes
- *June 8th, 2010:* Unemployment hits 10 percent

It seems like there was a crisis every minute reported in the financial media, but I'd rather not refresh your stress levels.

What amazes me most about the events from above is that each one was supposed to be the next "end-of-the-world-as-we-know-it." Capitalism, banking systems, and businesses that have propelled this country to the level of dominance in the world markets were no longer going to work— many have said it was all smoke and mirrors. But I believe they were wrong. Capitalism has been re-energized, banking systems are restructuring, and businesses have adapted by having some of the strongest balance sheets they have seen in over fifty years. And the government… well, we won't go there.

On the week of March 11th, 2008, the S&P 500 Index closed at around 1,256.98, and the week of January 7th, 2011, the S&P 500 Index closed at around 1,276.56 (and this does not include dividends). Many investors jumped out of the markets and into cash to wait out the onslaught of bad news but said they would get back in as soon as they *felt* comfortable that the current crisis was over. And many are still waiting.

Or you could take a lesson from Rip Van Winkle; by doing nothing (*only because he was sleeping and couldn't allow his emotions to get the best of him*) he may have potentially awoken to find his investment portfolio at a level similar to when he fell asleep.

To do so when you are awake requires a unique type of discipline, but you get my point.

Chapter Takeaways:

- Elite planners focus their time and attention toward attempting to control the critical variables—those variables that will most likely dictate the success of their clients' families' most cherished long-term, real-life goals.

- Planners help their clients embrace the three principles: Mindset, Patience and Discipline.

    - Mindset: If a person wakes up every day in constant fear that at any moment the world as they know it is on the brink of collapse (world events, politics, interest rates, war, the business cycle...blah, blah, blah) no matter how impeccable their plan or investments have been crafted to their unique lifelong dreams and desires, *they will blow it up.*

    - Patience: The siren song of the financial media—fueled by a need to generate "eyeball revenue or clickbait"—is tugging on your brain's weakness to—Just. Do. Something (financially speaking). For such times as these, we can find a calming truth from a hidden treasure of our childhood past. ***"Doing nothing often leads to the very best of something." – Winnie the Pooh***

    - Discipline: The act of not *reacting* and continue doing what has always worked requires restraint because you can't sleep through financial crises like a modern-day Rip Van Winkle.

The Practices

Systematic investing will pay off ultimately, provided that it is adhered to conscientiously and courageously under all market conditions.

– Ben Graham, Father of Value Investing

We now can begin the next phase, once we have understood and conquered the beasts within the brain using Mindset, Patience, and Discipline. As mentioned earlier, the practices become a natural progression, which can manifest into an investor's long-term, real-life returns required to provide the dignity and independence in a potential three-decade retirement. The best way to achieve this is to follow three practices: asset allocation, diversification, and rebalancing.

The first practice, *asset allocation*, simply refers to the percentage of equities versus bonds and cash in your portfolio over your investing lifetime. To most, this would seem like a very novel concept; however, this number—more than any other portfolio variable—will likely dictate the majority of your lifetime investment return. That is how critical this concept is to your financial success. Do NOT overlook it.

How can I make such an audacious statement? The answer is two-fold: 1) there have been numerous studies which verify this conclusion, and 2) it is countercultural.

First, the study.

The most recognized study was performed in a July/August 1986 paper entitled, "Determinants of Portfolio Performance," by Gary Brinson, L. Randolph Hood, and Gilbert Beebower from the *Financial Analysts Journal.* To summarize, it stated that on average, a portfolio's static target asset allocation accounted for some 93% of its variation of returns and volatility. The other 7% came from timing, selection and everything else other than asset allocation. If you think about it, it makes all the sense in the world, essentially stating how much an investor's allocation is dedicated to equities verses fixed investments (bonds and cash) provides the greatest impact on long-term returns.

At this point, you may be asking, "What is the recommended asset allocation I should have in my portfolio and does this study still hold true with our advancement in investment technology?" Understandable. Let's address the second thought from a quote from the legendary investor, Sir John Templeton who famously said, the four most dangerous words in investing are: "This Time is Different." Enough said.

The next area to address is the ideal asset allocation for your investment portfolio. It depends. Meaning, what are your unique cash flow needs (based on your financial plan), your comfort level with uncertainty (can you stomach the ups and downs of the markets), and your age. This brings us back to the prior conversation with the prospective clients who asked about what type of returns they could expect. Go ahead and re-read it on page 53. Although the answers to these three areas will dictate the allocation you should maintain, the answer to one (your comfort with uncertainty) is the key to long-term wealth.

Let's examine further. The long-term compound return of large-company stocks (equities) over the last roughly nine decades (since 1926) —with dividends reinvested—is about 10% annually. For small company stocks, the figure is around twelve percent, because of their higher volatility (*which most define as risk*). The compound return of long-term, corporate bonds—interest reinvested—is just a bit under six percent. And finally, long term government bonds—interest reinvested—is around five percent. Summarized (historically):

Nominal Returns (before inflation):

- Large Company Stocks: 10%
- Small Company Stocks: 12%
- Corporate Bonds: 6%
- Government Bonds: 5%

But wait. We are not done yet; these are nominal returns—meaning before we remove inflation (*remember the silent killer*). If you remove from these nominal returns the long-term inflation of around three percent, you're left with the *real returns*: the 7 and 9% that large and small company stocks have provided are historically compounding at two to three times the 3% real return of corporate and government bonds. This is a Grand Canyon of a gap when we are talking about the compounding of long-term returns. *Behold the simplicity of the Brinson Study.*

Real Returns (after inflation):

- Large Company Stocks: 7%
- Small Company Stocks: 9%
- Corporate Bonds: 3%
- Government Bonds: 2%

Why is this so countercultural? To explain, we will view it from the perspective of one of my all-time favorite movies, *The Godfather*. If you recall, there is a scene in the movie where they're all seated at the funeral of The Don, Vito Corleone. However, in a flashback, when Vito is still alive, Michael is talking to his father (Vito) in the garden and Vito tells Michael, "Remember, whoever comes to you with this meeting, he's the traitor, don't forget that."

Fast forward to all the organized crime families attending the funeral to pay their respects, and Michael, now head of the family, is surveying the landscape. Tom, the consigliere, leans over to Michael and says, "You know how they're going to come at you?" So, as your financial consigliere, I ask you—the average investor— "You know how they're going to come at you?" If you have been paying attention to the media, your response will probably be, "Timing and selection." Let's explore why that answer is so prevalent and why it's wrong.

As mentioned earlier, we live in a time of instant news, messages, texting, food, cash, and gratification. The American investor wants to *feel* as though they have all the available resources at their fingertips instantaneously. Armed with all of this information, investors *believe* that the solution to "superior investment performance" is timing and selection—as fed to them by the financial media and those businesses in that industry. They are the ones *asking for the meeting*.

In fairness, they are businesses and need to generate a profit—whether it be the mutual fund companies, rating services (Morningstar), or the media outlets. Although they have not come outright and said it, they have implied that the primary determinant of the investor's success is timing (when to be in or out of the markets) and selection (what specific investment you need to own now). Let us look at each source.

Morningstar is famous for their star system. They rate funds with either one star or as high as five stars; although, they have come out publicly to say that their ratings are only a guide for investors and all investors should look much deeper into other factors before choosing a mutual fund or exchange traded fund (ETF). However, human nature being as it is (cognitive heuristics), I would say this is about as far as most investors will venture—hence they have not stopped using the star system.

Mutual fund companies continue to advertise how many of their fund managers have four and five stars or have beaten the S&P 500 index over one, three, five and ten years. Again, actions speak louder than words or shall we say—inactions. Fund managers know very well how long-term wealth is accumulated and preserved, which is to continually add monies to a fund and not jump in and out based on the current years' stars. These advertisements promote jumping from one fund to the next.

Money Magazine, which I compassionately refer to as the *National Enquirer* of the financial industry, is always a favorite of mine. They have been publishing, each year for decades, headlines on the cover, such as "The Ten Hot Stocks/Bonds/ETFs/Gold/Oil/Real Estate/Funds (*input your assets class of the day*) You Must Own Today." By the way, if you go back to each prior year, you'll find that almost none of the prior years' funds show up on the current list. Shocker.

CNBC in its heyday, in the mid-to-late 1990's, would interview two talking heads with opposing prognostications. Bull (positive view) versus Bear (negative view) on the following topics: stocks vs bonds, gold vs dollar, growth vs value, economic outlook, government spending, corporate earnings, and recessions. However, I have yet to recall any conversation—even for a moment—about the following:

Over the long term, the success or failure of the average investor depends on how much they save and spend. And the dominant determinant of real-life returns that real people get is the behavior of the investor themselves.

Wow, how boring is that!

One final thought: if the media were to tell the investing public that the principles and practices I have described would determine as high as 93% of their long-term lifetime returns and all others (timing, selection) account for about 7%, they would most likely be out of business in less than six months.

The second practice is *diversification.* If asset allocation tells us what percentage of stocks/bonds/cash is ideal, diversification indicates what we should own within each asset class. For example, within the equity asset class you will need to decide what part of your investment goes into large or small company equities, domestic/developed world equities, or emerging markets. In addition, you might choose actively managed funds, indexed funds, or ETFs. Notice, I did not say individual stocks in any of these categories. Why? Because, as any truthful investor will tell you, nobody is near smart enough to track all information necessary to hold individual stocks.

A brief reasoning is most likely required here for buying individual stocks, which will illustrate the rationale for not building a portfolio of individual stocks as an individual investor. In full disclosure, when I began in the industry back in 1995 at Dean Witter (*yes, remember this name*), I would build client portfolios with—you guessed it—individual stocks.

At this time, it was all about how each Wall Street firm's research divisions, called stock analysts, would help guide brokers in building positions for their clients. It made sense to me, as I was a newbie in the industry, and this was how most senior brokers in the business were handling their clients. A confession: *Oh, how naive I was to believe in the company line.* Then, our firm was bought by what is known as the "white shoes" of the Wall Street firms.

We were told that they were *it* because their research departments (stocks analysts) only gave advice to the ultra-wealthy (*can you hear the harps playing in the background?*). I assumed they were going to dramatically help with investment recommendations for my clients. Unfortunately, over the next roughly 12-20 months I noticed something interesting: their recommendations or mutual funds they ran were no better (*in regard to performance*) than anyone else on Wall Street. And in many cases their analyst stock ratings were dead wrong. Here is where I will fully admit I fell prey to a classic behavioral bias, called authority bias.

What is authority bias? In his book, *Influence: The Psychology of Persuasion*, Robert Cialdini, PhD, and Regents' Professor Emeritus of Psychology and Marketing at Arizona State University, provides one of the most fascinating studies by a psychology professor, Stanley Milgram.

An ad was taken out in a local newspaper from a university, looking for participants in a "memory study." Participants arrived at the lab and after meeting with the researchers, it was explained that the study was about how punishment affects both learning and memory. One "learner" was to read and memorize pairs of words in a long sentence, until they would be able to memorize them perfectly. The other participant's job was to be the "teacher," who was told to administer small, but increasingly stronger electric shocks for every mistake.

After the learner would read the list of words and study for a small while, the researcher in the white jacket would strap the learner in a chair and hook electrodes to the learner's arm, as the teacher looked on. Inevitably, the learner would ask about the severity of the shocks. The researcher would answer that although shocks can be extremely painful, they will not cause permanent tissue damage. After the discussion, both the researcher and the teacher went into a different room to ask the learner to recite the sentence for the experiment.

The test proceeded with the teacher asking the questions and waiting for the responses from the learner. When a wrong answer was given, the teacher was instructed to call out the level of shock and pull a lever to administer the shock at an increasing rate of 15 volts per wrong answer. As the test progressed, the volts moved upward from uncomfortable, as witnessed by the teacher, but tolerable. However, as the wrong answers piled up, the pain increased. When the shocks hit 120 volts, the learner began to visibly flinch and tell the teacher, "It is beginning to really hurt." The teacher continued until 150-volts, when the learner screamed, "Stop, I can't take it anymore. I want to quit."

Now at a level of intolerable pain, most people would expect that the teacher and researcher would end the test—but almost all the subjects in the role of teacher proceeded to the next question.

The wrong answers continued, as the learner shrieked in pain, 195, 255, and 300 volts. Finally, the learner shouted out that he will no longer answer the questions, but most of the teachers responded to this response as a wrong answer and continue with the shocks, now up to a level of 400 volts.

So, did this actually happen? As Dr. Cialdini further explains, in most aspects it did. The only feature that was not real is that no physical shocks were delivered, and the "learner" was an actor who pretended to be screaming in pain. The participants in the study were placed in the *teacher role.*

The study was not about memory and punishment. *It was to study how much pain a normal human would inflict on another, when it was their job, with an authority figure present and providing instructions.*

In the study, nearly two-thirds of all participants who were in the teacher position pulled every one of the thirty shock switches, until the researchers ended the experiment. Even as it was applied, and the teachers were clearly uncomfortable (*sweating, jittered, dug their fingernails into flesh*) to a point of asking to stop the experiment, they did not disobey the authoritative figure.

Only a small percentage of the teachers pulling the lever at the 300-volt level stopped. The results of the experiment stunned just about all psychologists and Milgram himself, as to the level of obedience to authority.

The obvious question is what could allow us, as humans, to carry out such terrible tasks?

Milgram's answer was simple; he believed it was a deep-seated sense of duty to authority we all have. Think of these types of "authority" figures throughout history that have been a detriment or strong influence on society—dictators, governments, cults, and religions. Additional studies have been run on other areas of authority, such as a title given to a person or simply the clothing that is worn. All have influenced some type of obedience over a person. So be cognitive of these characteristics—I sure learned my lesson very quickly. In other words, don't let people who seem to have authority, like financiers, bankers, and television personalities, direct you to behaviors that do not contribute to your long-term goals. Instead, follow proven financial advice that is based on your unique financial plan which will guide you to diversify and protect yourself from unnecessary risk.

To complete the diversification discussion, author Nick Murray says it best, regarding what adequate diversification means:

"I'll never own enough of any one thing to make a killing in it; I'll never own enough of any one thing to get killed by it."

And the third practice is *rebalancing*. Rebalancing is not altering your portfolio every time the market changes, which is what many investors do. If you've followed the first two practices correctly, allocating your assets according to your financial plan and then diversifying further within each asset class, within a year, market fluctuations will redistribute your portfolio away from the original long-term percentage mix. For example, based on your plan, let's say we allocated 25% of your capital into each of four different equity categories (Large/Small/International/Emerging Markets). Then, one year later, some areas of the portfolio will have outperformed and others underperformed, relative to each other. Therefore, you now do not have four categories of 25% each but something like this: 35%/28%/20%/17%.

Unfortunately, what most investors have done is to sell what just temporarily went down and put the money into what just shot out the lights, thereby selling low and buying high (by the way, this is what happened in the late 1999's during the dot.com bubble). *If one genuinely wants to know how to underperform your planning needs for long periods of time—this is your winning formula.*

Rebalancing—which should be done on the same day or as close to the same day every year—is a planned adjustment in which investors sell some of the positions that just went up and add the capital (money) into things which are temporarily out of favor. Seems strange to say but yes, I will say it again, investors are *buying more of what did bad and selling what just did well*—this is as countercultural as it gets. And, may I add, a difficult concept for the brain to grasp—as I have had more conversations with clients about this than can be counted. I call this strategy *long-term investing*—as opposed to *short-term speculation.*

Since we are on the topic of investing versus speculating, a huge misconception for investors is believing they are investing when in fact they are speculating. We shall now break it down to its core: let me get this out in the open in all its hydra-headed forms. All market timing, forecasting, short-term trading, options, futures contracts, hedges and performance chasing are speculation. Do not kid yourself or allow some software system, cable show, or product salesperson try to convince you any different. It. Is. Speculating. Period.

There you have it—the beast of speculation is out of the cave, do with it as you will. Meaning, slay it or embrace it.

Chapter Takeaways:

- The practices become a natural progression, which can manifest into an investor's long-term, real-life returns required to provide dignity and independence in a potential three-decade retirement.

- *Asset Allocation* simply refers to the percentage of equities versus bonds and cash in your portfolio over your investing lifetime. To most, this would seem a very novel concept, however this number—more than any other portfolio variable—will likely dictate most of your lifetime investment return.

- The Brinson Study stated that on average, a portfolio's static target asset allocation accounted for some 93% of its variation of returns and volatility. The other 7% came from timing, selection, and everything else other than asset allocation.

- *Diversification* is as important as asset allocation. If asset allocation tells us what percentage of stocks/bonds/cash is ideal, diversification is indicating what we should own within each asset class.

- Author Nick Murray says it best, with regard to adequate diversification: "I'll never own enough of any one thing to make a killing in it; I'll never own enough of any one thing to get killed by it."

- *Rebalancing*—which is done on the same day or at least the same month every year—is a planned adjustment in which investors sell some of the positions that just went up and add the capital into things which are temporarily out of favor. Seems strange to say but yes, I will say it again, investors are *buying more of what did bad and selling what just did well*—this is as countercultural as it gets.

- Investing vs Speculating involves a huge misconception for investors who often believe they are investing when in fact they are speculating. We shall now break it down to its core: let me get this out in the open in all its hydra-headed forms. All market timing, forecasting, short-term trading, options, futures contracts, hedges and performance chasing are speculation. Do not kid yourself or allow some software system, cable show, or product salesperson try to convince you any different. It. Is. Speculating. Period.

The Portfolio

Those who have persisted with equities have always been rewarded. No one has made money in the long run from betting against stocks or the future growth of our economy.

-Jeremy J. Siegel, Professor of Finance The Wharton School, author of Stocks for the Long Run

Ah, yes. This is what everyone has been waiting for—The Portfolio. Like a concert that you attended when you had to patiently endure the warm-up band before you got to the main event. As was The Plan, now you are at The Portfolio. I understand, just admit it...you will not hurt my feelings.

The one characteristic planners, those worth multiples of their value provided, all have in common is that we are somewhat callused. Not in a negative way, just that we do not take anything personally because we've learned long ago that we are not looking for outcomes or trying to prove anything to clients/prospective clients. We are fully aware we are here to steward the ship to financial freedom—however that is defined by each family—to those finite numbers who are willing to embrace it (*yes, a confession of a planner*). In plain English, we provide the way and let the chips fall where they may because we cannot want more for the financial well-being of a family than they want for themselves.

Before any portfolio can be built, the investor needs to understand how each component of the portfolio works. For example, if you were to build a house, you need to know a hammer's, wrench's, and screw drivers' primary functions. You would not use a wrench to pound in a nail (well, most would not) or a hammer to drill in a screw. Each tool has a purpose and when that tool is not used for its primary purpose, eventually over time or in extreme stormy weather, the house will collapse.

When it comes to investing, the investor's primary tools are stocks (fractional ownership of businesses), bonds (a lender to the business) and Treasury Bills (debt issued by the government) and cash. Yes, I know there are other areas to invest but these have been the investor's core tools as far back as 1802. Understand that each component is critical to the average investor's long-term investment success. And the best way for investors to comprehend the functionality of each is by comparing it to its volatility, as I mentioned in prior conversations, and how it relates to inflation in providing a real return. Stay with me here…it will become completely clear soon.

The graph below provides a comprehensive view of how each asset class has performed since 1802. If one ever wanted to know, in detail, the history of the markets and how each asset class has reacted in different time periods, this is *the* book.

Defined below (Total Real Return Indexes), stocks are represented by Large Company Stocks, Bonds are High Quality Corporate, Bills are represented by Government Treasury Bills, Gold, and finally the Dollar (*remember our story of the mattress—that's how I know*). And as a reminder, if we want to know the nominal return of each asset class, just add a rate of inflation to each percentage below, if it makes you feel better.

Total Real Return Indexes

This chart shows the long-term cumulative growth of $1 from major asset classes, as well as the average annual real returns that accumulate to those long-term wealth gains.

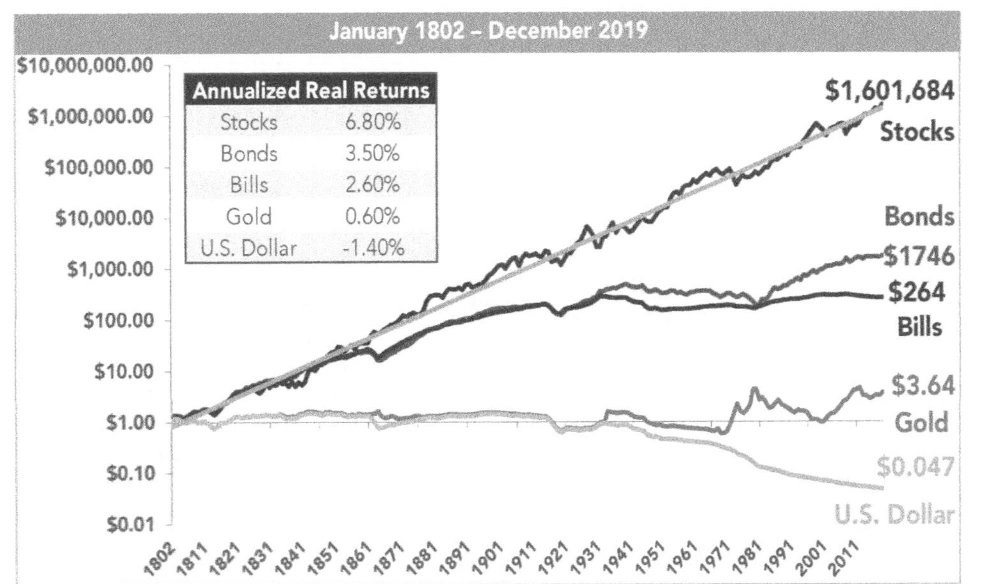

Source: Siegel, Jeremy, Stocks for the Long Run (2014), with updates to 2019. Past performance is not indicative of future results.

While we are here in this discussion, let us conquer the mother of all misperceptions—*stocks are risky, and bonds are safe*—by viewing another chart from Mr. Siegel's handy fact-driven book titled: *Holding Period Returns for Each Asset Class.*

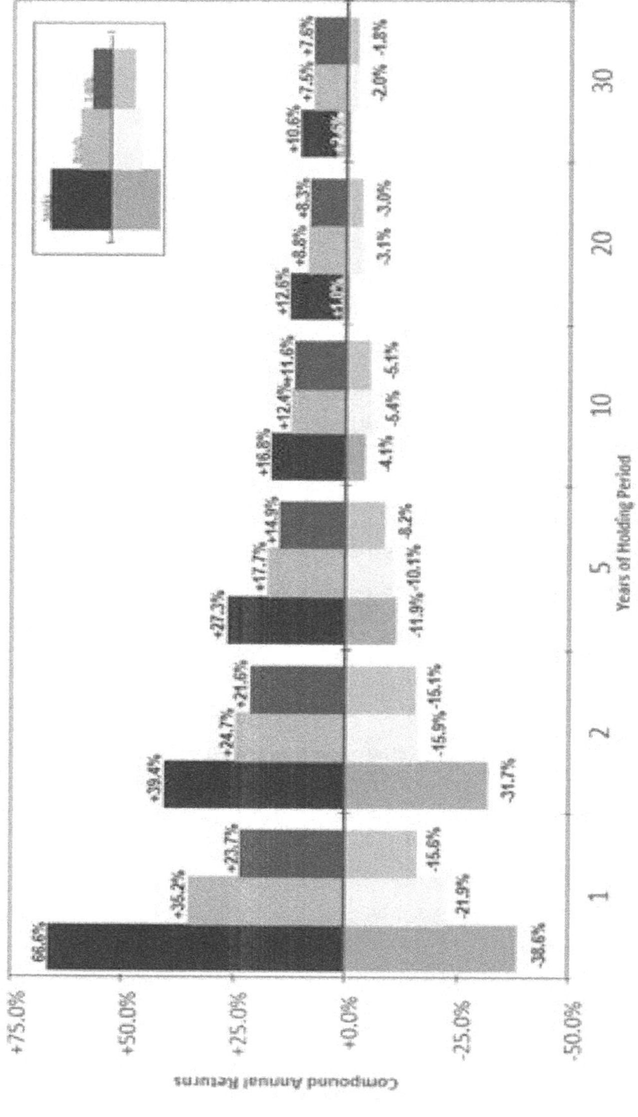

Copyright Jeremy J. Siegel.
Source: Siegel, Jeremy, Stocks for the Long Run (2014), With Updates to 2019.

What you are seeing above is the reality that nobody in the media will EVER begin to reveal and quite frankly, a terrifying concept for most retirees to wrap their emotional brain around. What are we looking at?

On the bottom line is the time frame; one-, two-, five-, ten-, twenty-, and thirty-year time periods since 1802. The percentages on the top and bottom of each bar represent the best and worst that asset's class has provided over that time frame—this is called volatility (most call it risk) or variability of the return. We are focused on Stocks, Bonds, and T-bills for the asset classes.

If we look at the one-year period, what do you see? What should stand out to you is the large swings (*highs and lows*) that each asset class provides. For example, Stocks have moved up as high as 66.6% and off as low as – 38.6% in a calendar year since 1802. Bonds have been up 35.2% and off – 21.9%, while T-Bills have been up 23.7% and off – 15.6%. Again, these are real returns—after the silent killer in retirement takes a bit—that real people get in real life, after inflation.

Are you with me on this? Because where I am driving the car is countercultural. It takes those "rules of thumb" the media provides, as one moves closer to retirement, and turns them upside down. In other words, the common belief that the average couple moving into retirement should begin to shift a large portion of their portfolio to bonds for both income production and less volatility is just not true (once the average couple understands money as purchasing power and that life expectancies will continue to rise, the wisdom begins).

Now, move your eyeballs to the right and begin to "see"—for the first time—the effects over longer time frames of what happens to each asset class's "swings" of returns. Get where I am going? Read again and look at the bars once you see the ten-year time frame and greater, as something very magical happens.

What has now been revealed, beginning at the ten-year time frame, is that the temporary down of stocks has now become less (or better) than those of bonds and T-Bills. Yes, this is after inflation. You now may want to brace yourself for the next two things I am about to reveal from the history of these asset classes from 1802-2019. Go ahead, sit if you will and take a deep breath. Are you seated? Okay, good.

Here we go: The *worst* real return over any twenty-year time frame since 1802 that stocks have provided has NEVER been negative. Never. And as you move even further to the thirty-year time frame It. Gets. Even. Better. Are you still seated? Or did you lose your breath, or did you fall off your chair?

But what about bonds?

You may need to take another deep breath for this one or maybe have your favorite cocktail in hand. Okay, here we go. What has been the real return on bonds over those same time frames? Before you answer this, let's go back and remember our discussion. We are speaking to the suitcase carrier who will be looking at what period of retirement, for an average life expectancy of a non-smoking couple? Thirty years. The worst real return of Bond/T-Bills over any twenty – or thirty-year period *still has a negative in it.*

Here comes the obvious slow ball down the middle—you know what the next question is? So, what asset class is the *riskiest* when it comes to a two-person, thirty-year retirement after factoring in *the silent killer*? BONDS. Viola. I know you are shocked those words just fell out of your mouth, as the beginning of wisdom can be astounding to most who were fooled by their misperceptions and then reinforced by the financial media. *The curtain has now fallen…the wizard of OZ has now been revealed.*

Take a minute, if you need, to grasp this overwhelming enlightenment of how long-term wealth is truly created and preserved for generations.

Before we go any further (*you may need another drink at this point*), you are probably saying, "So, you're recommending we place everything we have in stocks at retirement?" NO. That is not what I said. I am simply pointing out what Sgt. Joe Friday (played by Dan Ackroyd) in the *Dragnet* movie said, "All we want are the facts, ma'am."

As I have mentioned, to build a beautifully diversified portfolio, we need to grasp how each tool works—historically. Unbiased and without distortion from any media source (wouldn't this be nice for all areas of our lives?). Only then, can the foundation be constructed for a diversified portfolio tied to the lifestyle-sustaining cash flow needs of the retired couple's financial plan using a portfolio which is required to last up to three decades and beyond.

Taking this to the next logical step, any successful long-term investment strategy must adhere to a comprehension of both principles and practices from the investor. If not followed, it will not only devastate the investor, but the portfolio will be pushing up daisies in short order, as the next inevitable crisis hits.

Now that you know how each tool works, let's build the portfolio for retirement.

Since the brain prefers to categorize how money is spent, called *mental accounting*, the proper way to build a portfolio is what can be described in our industry as goals/needs-based planning. Or visually think of it as buckets to place your dollars into, based on your goals/needs and their time frame.

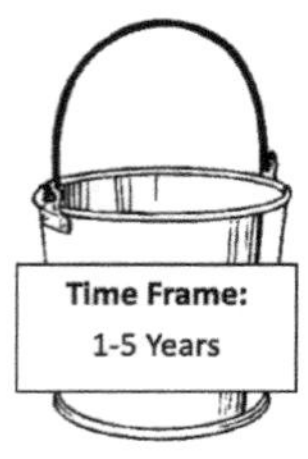

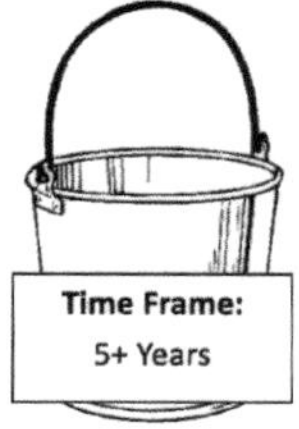

The first bucket is your emergency monies, those are set aside into the zero-to-twenty-four-month timeframe. These funds are to be used when (*not if*) the market takes its normal bear market dip about once every five years. How much is in this bucket you may ask? Well, how nervous—meaning how much can you stomach the temporary dip—of an investor are you and your family? It can be from six months to twenty-four months of living expenses.

The second bucket is for any large items (boat, roof repair, vacation, wedding) that was or is planned to happen in the next five years. These are dollars that need to be there for a set time frame to cover a known cost. We want to make sure they are not exposed to the day-to-day fluctuations of the equity markets revealed in the prior charts.

The third and final bucket is for long-term investment planning and wealth accumulation, which is tied directly to the comprehensive financial plan you and your CERTIFIED FINANCIAL PLANNER™ crafted and will annually update.

Once the actual process is in motion, our conversation continues:

SC Carrier: *Now that we are retiring, we're not really comfortable putting all of our money into the market. What if it goes down? We don't have the time or desire to go back to work until it recovers.*

Planner: *Yes, this can be a very anxious time for both of you. I understand.*

SC Carrier: *What do you recommend we do? You just mentioned a moment ago that we've had a "bear market" about once every five years since the end of WWII. How would we recover from that if it happened tomorrow, and if we need that money?*

Planner: *If you will, look at these three buckets. One is for living expenses, one is for any item you know you'll need to purchase or fund in the next five years, and the last bucket is for long-term growth to provide you both with the lifestyle-sustaining income we've discussed in the plan.*

SC Carrier: *OK. What goes in those buckets?*

Planner: *Let's go over it. The first bucket is going to be invested in either a money market or your local savings account. It will have about 13 months of living expenses, based on what our plan told us. Think of this bucket as a "night-light" for emotional safety. Although we're not getting a good return on those monies, it's okay, because that's not this bucket's purpose.*

Its primary purpose—when the bear market or whatever crisis of the day hits—is to keep those normal emotions from driving you to behave yourselves out of the third bucket's purpose. Hence, a night-light in stormy weather.

SC Carrier: *You mean we can live on these monies when it gets really ugly?*

Planner: *Yes. What typically happens during a normal correction or regular bear market (again this is a 20% drop or greater) is that a sense of fear blankets most investors. Again—piled high and deep by the media—and it triggers a fear that this temporary down is going to become a permanent loss of your investments.*

Using market history as our guide, which is the only thing we must rely on, I can say that I don't know ***when*** *it will stop dropping but I know it* ***will*** *stop dropping. However, when you're both in the midst of the storm, I've done this long enough to realize that any rational facts I give at that moment will matter* ***zero*** *when your emotions are in full force.*

Simply said, fear does not care about facts.

SC Carrier: *Oh, yeah, that lifeboat drill you were talking about earlier. I have to admit, I've let that fear get to me before.*

Planner: *Exactly. And we've already discussed the purpose for the second bucket. Again, don't confuse this fixed income (bond) bucket with the goal of providing income for our living expenses. It's a side perk, but our primary goal is for both of you not to be looking at your daughter just before the wedding ceremony and saying, "Honey, our investments have been down lately, so how about that accordion player at Uncle Fester's wedding instead of the band you requested?"*

Probably not a good conversation. So, let's not take any chances.

SC Carrier: *Ha-Ha...that's pretty funny...do you have a cheaper band? Just kidding (looking nervously at his spouse).*

Planner: *Now the third bucket. This bucket's primary goal is for long-term total return, over a five-year or longer timeframe. It's a diversified equity portfolio built for your cash flow needs, according to your comprehensive financial plan.*

SC Carrier: *Ok, but don't bonds provide more income in retirement than stocks?*

One of the most deceiving and destructive misperceptions for the retiree—*the beast* has just performed a back flip from the suitcase and smacked its head on your table. Kerplunk. This is best explained with the chart below (Dividends Historically Provide More Income Than Bonds on The Same Invested Amount) providing a snapshot of a thirty-year time frame from 1988 to 2018:

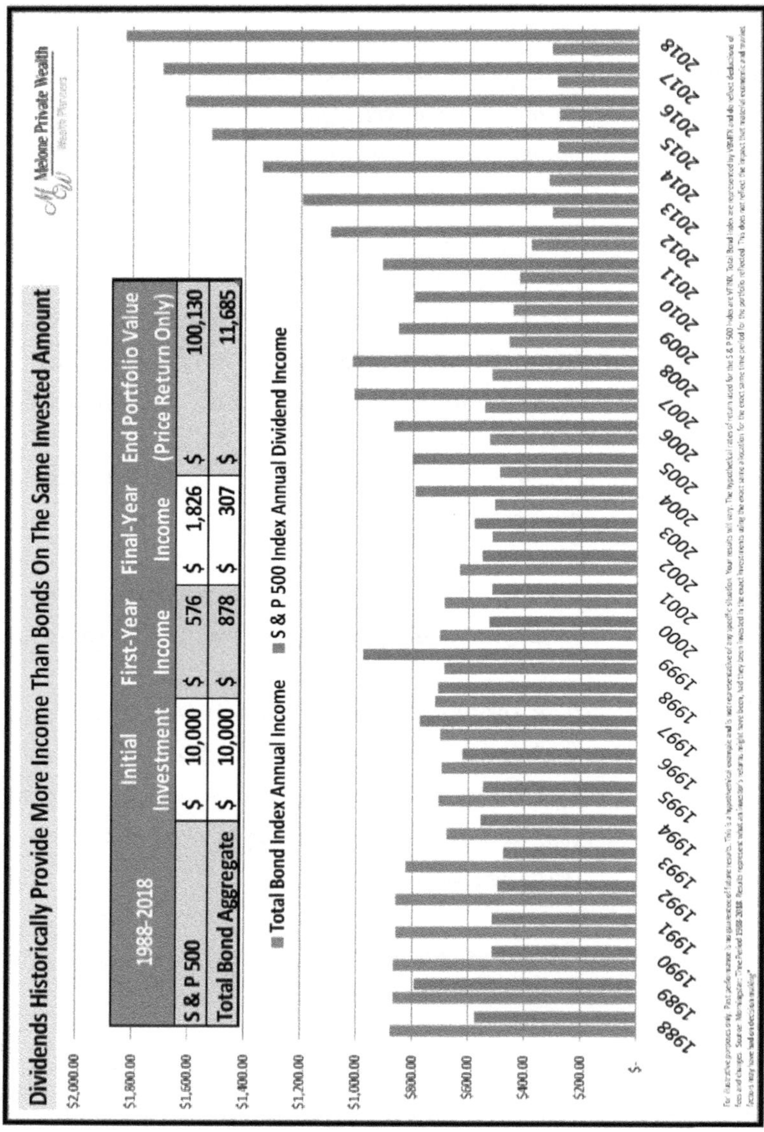

1988-2018	Initial Investment	First-Year Income	Final-Year Income	End Portfolio Value (Price Return Only)
S & P 500	$ 10,000	$ 576	$ 1,826	$ 100,130
Total Bond Aggregate	$ 10,000	$ 878	$ 307	$ 11,685

What you are witness to in the above chart is the following (in each time period at the bottom, it displays Total Bond Index on the left and S & P 500 on the right):

Two hypothetical investors, each invest $10,000 beginning in 1988. The conservative investor (in their mind) needs income and decides, with the old myths well at hand, he will place the entire $10,000 into bonds, represented by the Total Aggregate Bond Index. He receives $878 of interest the first year.

The other investor, who would be considered more aggressive, by myth standard, decides to invest all $10,000 into stocks, represented by the S&P 500 index. She receives $576 in dividend income the first year.

At this point, the conservative investor is feeling extremely comfortable getting the 8.78% interest on the bond index investment. Conversely, the aggressive investor is only getting 5.76% in dividend yield on the stock index investment. However, as mentioned multiple times throughout this book, *retirement planning is not about what you are getting in income over one year but throughout the potential thirty years in retirement. All while trying to fight off a silent killer of retirement—inflation.*

Fast forward thirty years. Now, the conservative investor is getting $307 or 3.07% interest income on the original $10,000. During the same period, the aggressive investor is getting (go ahead, say it with me) $1,826 per year in dividend income or 18.26% dividend income on the original $10,000 invested.

Not to rub salt in the gash, but since we are standing above the beast of misconception on the table, ready to put it out of its misery, why not? The principal growth of the original $10,000 over the thirty-year period has now become what amount for each retiree?

The conservative investor received a bit over $11,000 back in principal. However, the aggressive investor received a bit over $100,000 back in principal. I don't think anyone needs a PhD in mathematics to realize the massive difference in those two real-life dollars. Are. We. Done. Here? Well, not really. There's more to learn.

Would you agree this beast has been laid to rest?

Investment success is based on three principles: Mindset, Patience, and Discipline. Flat out, if you cannot stomach the temporary downs equities (stocks) provide historically, you will never be a successful long-term investor. Period. Sorry to be the messenger of reality, but this is the truth. Which is why the buckets (goals/needs-based planning) are used, as a guide to temper the emotional mind, while the beast tries to climb back into the suitcase.

Let us finish the retirement income withdrawal process conversation.

SC Carrier: *(after planner explains the above process) We never thought of it that way. I don't think anyone has ever explained it to us before.*

Planner: *Not surprising. It's countercultural.*

SC Carrier: *Ok. So, we have all our buckets filled, based on our planning needs. What happens when the average bear market drops of 30% hits?*

Planner: *Again, we are drawing around 4.5% per year off this third bucket to live on. Remembering that each year we increase that dollar amount we draw by inflation around 3%—to fight the rising cost of living.*

Then the bear hits (or some other crisis) —one that is more along the average time and drop since the end of WWII: around 30% and lasting for about 13 months. We can turn off all withdraws and reset all our holdings to dividend reinvest. At the same time, we now turn on bucket number one, with our two years of living expenses, and begin to live on it.

SC Carrier: *Makes sense. I like the concept and it's easy to understand, which makes us feel better. What if it drops further or lasts longer?*

Planner: *It's very possible that this will happen. There are modifications we can look at to battle this possibility, but as I mentioned before, anything is possible, but we can only plan on the probable. Which is why we kept up to two years of living expenses in bucket one—even though 13 months is roughly the average time frame of these bear market drops since the end of WWII.*

SC Carrier: *Oh, now we get it. So, if we wanted to be more exact based on these events and the probabilities—it would be 13 months.*

Planner: *Now you both are understanding how planning truly works. Welcome to the beginning of Wisdom.*

To summarize:

- Set aside up to two years of living expenses in a money market fund.
- Add the known future one-time purchases into fixed income (bonds).
- Invest the rest into a diversified equity portfolio.
- Begin to withdraw from the equity portfolio about 4.5% per year from both dividends and principal gain.
- Each successive year increase the dollar amount to withdraw by about 3% per year to offset the rise in cost of living (inflation).

What I would like to address here is akin to the scene in the *Godfather* when Michael goes to meet with Sollozzo in the Italian Restaurant, while accompanied by the Police Chief, McCluskey. Sollozzo looks at McCluskey and says, "I'm going to speak Italian to Michael." Similarly, I am going to speak "Financial-ese" for those PhDs in math and planners who are reading my "buckets" approach for a method of withdrawal.

The "4% Rule" is a greatly debated topic in the financial planning inner circles. There are those who will say this process may not work because the back-testing of the results (when using different mixes of portfolios between stocks and bonds) may only provide a success rate of about 85% of the time. In addition, it may not address the potential issue of the "sequence of returns" risk for those retirees who begin to withdraw at the onset of retirement if a normal bear market occurs immediately. Which is very real.

First, in what world does certainty exist? Other than in the minds of those who are driven to have exact results in some financial laboratory. For those of us who live in and survive in the real world of planning for probabilities, I would call the "concern of only 85%" a high probability. And I never said it would work 100% of the time, but it does not have to for clients to not run out of money. What I know, from applying the process over twenty-five years with real people in the real world, is it has worked in the majority of cases. Not 100%, but darn close to it.

When it did not, in those few cases it was mainly due to an over-spending issue, so we had an adult planning conversation between the client and planner to make some adjustments. Then the retirement train was back on its tracks for future generations to ride. Again, annual planning updates in the real world with counsel from those planners who adapt to life events. As I have stated in the past, a client's plan is a living breathing document that changes, as life events will inevitably change.

Secondly, I'm highly skeptical that a perfect withdrawal formula exists. Why? Because what has worked in the past is in the past. As much as one PhD wants to speak PhD to another PhD and congratulate themselves for solving some mind-numbing formula *they* can only understand—who's to say the future will hold the same set of back-tested inputs? Sorry, but I have witnessed way too many "back-tested" theories that are later found to be faulty. Can anyone say, "Credit Default Swaps" or "Collateral Debt Obligations" during the 2000 Housing Crisis? Or how about the Black-Scholes model that was used to create "Portfolio Insurance" during the 1987 Black Monday Crash? All were built on assumptions.

As stated in his book, *A History of the United States in Five Crashes* by Scott Nations:

> …very few people understand the essence of the models. But the world of mortgage-backed securities had convinced itself that the Gaussian copula model allowed them to understand all the risks in mortgage securities, even though Li warned, "The most dangerous part is when people believe everything coming out of it…"

Finally, we as planners need to face the simple fact that there is and will always be ambiguity in just about any and all withdrawal formulas proposed to any clients. However, by applying the bucket process for clients as discussed in the conversation above, we have been successful in that all clients have grown and preserved a legacy for generations to come. That is my proof, and I will stand by it. This concludes the section for what I call "those who want to know how the watch works (the PhDs teaching formulas)" verses just knowing what time it is (the average retiree).

The Power of Compounding

Compound interest is the 8th wonder of the world. He who understands it, earns it. He who doesn't pays it.

-Albert Einstein

I would be remiss if I didn't touch on and point out an often discussed and very underestimated tool to build long-term wealth—compounding. One of the reasons, I believe, it is such an underestimated tool can be attributed to our current culture—one that feeds on the minute-by-minute reactions the average investor exhibits to meaningless events. All served up daily by the media.

The second reason is human nature—or more to the point—our brain's inability to visualize many concepts into the future. According to Jane McGonigal in the article titled, "Our Puny Human Brains are Terrible at Thinking About the Future," dated April 13, 2017,

...fMRI studies suggest that when you imagine your future self, your brain does something weird: It stops acting as if you're thinking about yourself. Instead, it starts acting as if you're thinking about a completely different person.

She continues with the study of functional magnetic resonance imaging (fMRI) and how it works when thinking about yourself when a part of the brain called the medial prefrontal cortex (MPFC) lights up. However, when thinking about other people or someone you don't know, it goes dark. What McGonigal is explaining is that the further in the future you're imagining yourself, *the less the fMRI activates.*

So how does this relate to long-term planning? It makes it harder for us to take actions for our future financial self. As stated by UCLA researcher Hal Ersner-Hershfield, "Why would you save money for your future self when, to your brain, it feels like you're just handing away your money to a complete stranger?" There are other implications to this beyond financial planning, such as reduced self-control, less ability to resist temptation, increased procrastination, lower motivation to exercise, a tendency to give up sooner when frustrated, and less likelihood to care about long-term challenges.

Getting back to concept of compounding power, those who have displayed the ability to grasp this concept have been granted tremendous wealth-building momentum. The king of this concept is Warren Buffett, as explained in an article by Jason Zweig published in the *Wall Street Journal* on August 28, 2020 titled, "Warren Buffett and the $300,000 haircut," as Mr. Buffett recently turned age 90.

> … The chairman of Berkshire Hathaway Inc. is one of the most successful investors of all time, having amassed a net worth estimated at $82 billion. Yet he accrued nearly 90% of that sum after the age of 65.… From the earliest age, Mr. Buffett has understood that building wealth depends not only on how much your money grows, but also on how long it grows.
>
> Around the age of 10, he read a book about how to make

> $1,000 and intuitively grasped the importance of time. In five years, $1,000 earning 10% would be worth more than $1,600; 10 years of 10% growth would turn it into nearly $2,600; in 25 years, it would amount to more than $10,800; in 50 years, it would compound to almost $117,400...
>
> His friends and family regularly heard the young Mr. Buffett mutter things like, "Do I really want to spend $300,000 for this haircut?" or "I'm not sure I want to blow $500,000 that way" when pondering whether to spend a few bucks. To him, a few dollars spent that day represented hundreds of thousands of dollars forgone in the future because they couldn't compound.
>
> Recognizing that every dollar you spend today is $10 or $100 or $1,000 you won't have in the future doesn't have to make you a miser. It teaches you to acknowledge the importance of measuring trade-offs. You should always weigh the need or desire that today's spending fulfills against what you could accomplish with that money after letting it grow for years or decades into the future.

This is the essence of an opportunity cost, which is the loss of one opportunity (compounded interest) due to choosing an alternative (making a purchase). For those of you who need to visualize what an opportunity cost is, below (provided by Invesco) is a sample of what it would be like to invest the cost of a cup of coffee over longer time periods, instead of ingesting it. By the way, did you ever think someone could spend over $43,000 on coffee?

The Opportunity Cost of Drinking a Small Coffee Every Day (Ingest) vs. Investing that Money*

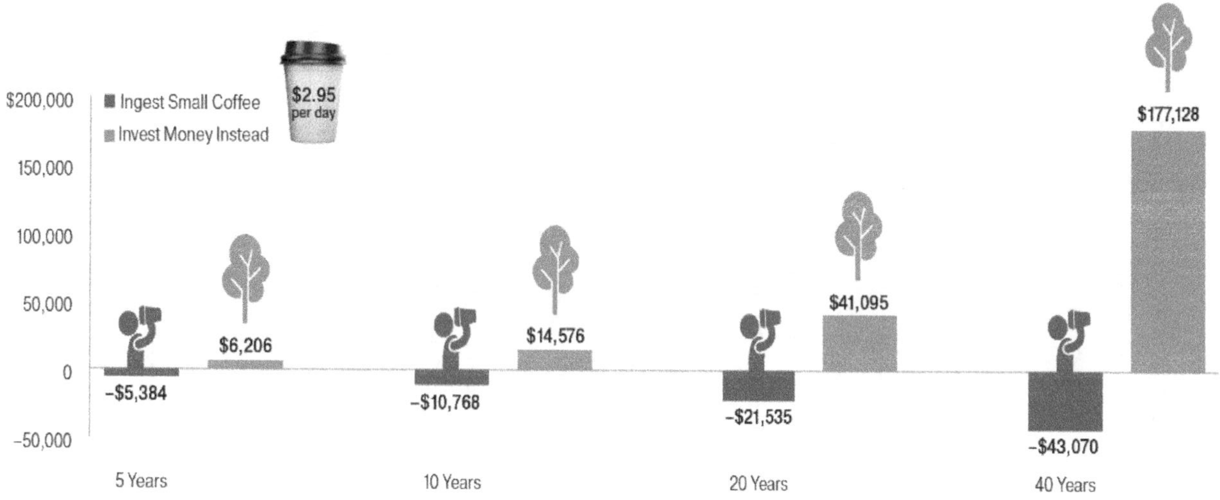

Ingest Small Coffee
Invest Money Instead

$2.95
per day

$200,000
150,000
100,000
50,000
0
-50,000

	Ingest Small Coffee	Invest Money Instead
5 Years	–$5,384	$6,206
10 Years	–$10,768	$14,576
20 Years	–$21,535	$41,095
40 Years	–$43,070	$177,128

* Investing assumes a 6% market return. 6% market return is based on a hypothetical mathematical example, not the performance of any market. For simplicity, this scenario assumes consistent returns for every year. Actual market returns are highly variabl which would negatively affect a portfolio's ending value when compared with consistent returns. Slide is for illustrative purposes only.

Finally, and straight to the point, allow the magic of compounding to happen, even though your brain is battling you every step of the way. The benefits are clear from the simple chart below, provided by Invesco, of four (4) individuals investing $12,500 annually until age 65, all beginning at a different age.

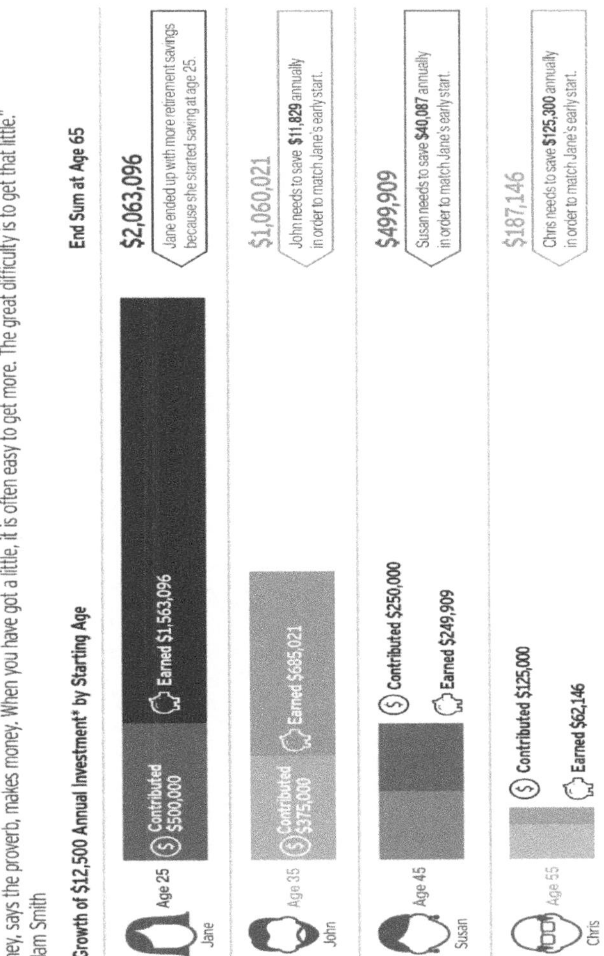

The Anatomy of Investor Returns

"Between stimulus and response, there is a space.
In that space, is our power to choose our response.
In our response, lies our growth and our freedom."

– *Viktor Frankl, author of* Man's Search for Meaning

The year is 1635 in Holland. The market price for tulip bulbs has skyrocketed, with the highest price attached to the rare "Semper Augustus." The price, thirty-thousand Florins or three times the value of an Amsterdam House at that time. Tulip Mania had arrived, then it crashed, and the price plunged to four hundred florins. This was the first modern bubble market, almost four hundred years ago.

As a brief history of bubbles and crashes:

- The South Sea Bubble in England during the 1720's
- The Mississippi Bubble in France during the 1720's

- In the United States, market bubbles and meltdowns have occurred since the nation's founding; some examples are the panics of 1785, 1792, five more in the 1800's and the crashes of 1929, 1967, 1987, 2000, and the great recession of 2008.

As distinct as each one is, the psychology that drives investors is always essentially the same; investor behavior is triggered by some form of stimulus—either a geo-political event, previous market experience, news stories, or a tip from a colleague/family member that distracts investors from their long-term goals. As a result, the investor reacts emotionally (*sometimes unconsciously*) and blows up their long-term financial plan and portfolio, which may never recover.

Let's witness a real-life conversation, when one of these crises occurs with a new client—as it will normally take a few of these events before the client will grasp the concepts we've discussed in our original meeting. Furthermore, as thorough as our conversations were when bringing on the new client, the beast in the suitcase will always try to reappear from time to time throughout the planner/client relationship.

We now join the conversation with said crisis in motion—with red tooth and pointy claws ready to pounce:

Planner: *Don't do that. I understand, but don't do that—you'll regret it.*

Client: *(with panic in his/her voice) Do you realize what they're saying and how this could impact my portfolio? If this crisis (insert event: COVID-19, Trade*

War, Presidential Elections, Brexit, Great Recession, 9/11, Tech Bubble, Russian Bond Default, Asian Contagion) happens, the markets will crash, and I'll lose a lot of money. At my age, it would take a long time to get it back…if ever.

Planner: *I understand. And it's ok to feel concerned about this event, but what we don't want to do is* ***react*** *to those feelings and allow this temporary dip, no matter how long, to become a permanent loss.*

Client: *But the news has this guy from (expert bank/Wall Street brokerage firm who is an economist/strategist) saying the market will crash and will take years to recover. It really feels different this time.*

Planner: *(empathetically, but sternly) How many of these "end-of-the-world-as-we-know-it" events have you and I gone through over the past handful of years?*

Client: *Well, uh, I guess a few, but this one is NOT like the others. The guy…*

Planner: *(interrupting the pattern of fear) Yes. We. Have. And…*

Client: *They've all worked out—but we're older now and we just don't have the time to recover if it gets as bad as they say it will.*

Planner: *I understand your concern. We both know from past experiences, when we're in the middle of the crisis, it* ***always feels*** *different…but it never IS differ-*

ent. The event may have a different name to it or a slightly different concern, but the emotional and market responses always remain the same—since Noah was looking for tar to caulk his boat.

Client: *Ha-Ha. Yeah, you've said this before. We can recall that from the last crisis a few years ago.*

Planner: *And that's why we have those buckets in place from our plan. If you would like me to, we can revisit them and while we're at it, let's look at your comprehensive plan to verify we're still on path to financial freedom as you've both described it to me.*

We will now investigate the science of decision-making, historical investor returns, and my personal "working lab" of twenty-five years advising real-life investors and their behavior, to present a model called "The Anatomy of Investor Returns."

To begin, do you know what the historical returns are that the average investor receives?

As discussed earlier, since 1994, DALBAR, an independent research firm, has revealed its Quantitative Analysis of Investor Behavior (QAIB) that measures the effects of investor decisions to buy, sell, and switch into and out of mutual funds over short – and long-term timeframes.

These effects are measured from the perspective of the investor and don't represent the performance of the investments themselves. The results have consistently shown that the average investor earns less—in many cases, much less —than mutual fund performance reports suggest.

For the 30-year period ending in 2019, these are the returns as follows.

S&P 500 Index	Average Equity Fund Investor
9.96%	**5.04%**

And since we are a more visual society, let's look at the same above data this way:

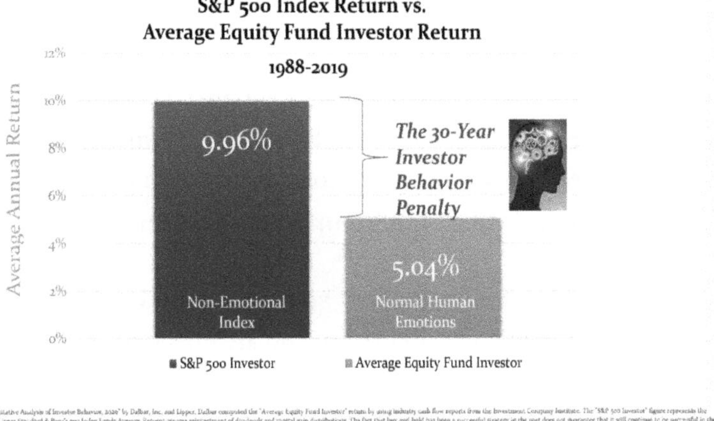

The best way to explain the behavioral gap in the above chart is with a real-life story from a person in the early 1950's, while working at the RAND Corporation, who became intrigued by a common financial question: how much of his retirement savings should he invest in the stock market?

He later published a mathematical equation that could be used to calculate the "optimal mix" of assets to figure out how to get the greatest return, for the optimal amount of risk in the portfolio. The formula later won him a Nobel Prize in Economics for an equation called Modern Portfolio Theory (MPT).

Who was this person? His name was Harry Markowitz.

What is most fascinating is not the egg-heady mathematical formula he was able to create, but that when asked later how he divided up his own portfolio, he admitted he ignored the investment model that won him that Nobel Prize. Why? He said he was so concerned with the amount of regret (*a cognitive bias*) he might feel later if he found out that the one he liked did worse than the one he didn't that he split his portfolio equally between stocks and bonds.

In effect, he behaved himself out of the long-term returns he could have received. Again, he could not bring himself, emotionally, to use his own theory, according to the interview in *The Monitor* with Professor Meir Statmen of May/June 2005.

Does this make him irrational or normal? I would call him a normal investor, just like all others who are affected by both cognitive bias and emotions.

Returning to our chart. *What you're witnessing from DALBAR is behavioral, specifically how the average investor behaves when all logic goes out the window, as one of the inevitable crises occurs.*

Although the actual numbers will move back and forth, based on the timeframe presented, the relationship between the two figures which I refer to as the Investor Behavior Penalty remains consistent. And if you have not picked up on the most glaring issue, let me point it out: the average equity fund investor has given away close to 50% of their potential returns over a 30-year period.

A word of caution: You may, after gazing at the graphic and reading the massive gap between the S&P 500 Index return and the average equity fund investor return, conclude that I am an advocate of passive investing over active investing. If so, you are missing the primary issue: It is INVESTOR BEHAVIOR.

As stated by the legendary advisor to advisors, Nick Murray: "The **dominant determinant** of **long-term, real-life investment** outcomes is not **investment performance** but **investor behavior.**" So, what does he mean by this in plain English? He essentially says *behavior is dominant*: it is more important than all other determinants put together. And *long-term, real-life portfolio returns*—the actual results real people really get—are only marginally affected by the relative performance of investments. Rather, they are *absolutely driven* by the behavior of investors.

Pause here for a moment and read this again because your family's success, as it pertains to long-term wealth accumulation and leaving a meaningful legacy to those you cherish most, depends on your commitment and capacity to embrace it.

Again, how does this continually happen with today's information and technology to educate investors at an all-time high? We need to refer to Behavioral Finance and Neurosciences for guidance.

Andrew W. Lo, a Professor of Finance and the Director of the Laboratory for Financial Engineering at the MIT Sloan School of Management Neuroscientists, explains:

> For example, monetary gain stimulates the same reward circuitry as cocaine—in both cases, dopamine is released into the nucleus accumbens. Similarly, the threat of financial loss apparently activates the same fight-or-flight response as a physical attack, releasing adrenaline and cortisol into the bloodstream, resulting in elevated heart rate, blood pressure, and alertness. These reactions are hardwired into human physiology, and while we're often able to overcome our biology through education, experience, or genetic good luck during normal market conditions, under more emotionally charged circumstances, the majority of the human population will behave in largely predictable ways.

In further excerpts from Professor Lo's white paper, he explains that studying individuals with brain tumors, lesions, or other head injuries has provided researchers with further data. One of the most notorious cases was of a young New Hampshire man named Phineas Gage, who had an iron rod pass under his upper jaw and through the top of his head during a rock-blasting accident in the construction of the Rutland & Burlington Railroad in 1848.

Gage survived and recovered, but his personality and habits changed. Later his doctor wrote that before the accident, Gage was "a shrewd, smart businessman, very energetic and persistent in executing all his plans of operation." After the accident, however, Gage was "impatient of restraint or advice when it conflicts with his desires, at times pertinaciously obstinate, yet capricious and vacillating, devising many plans of future operations, which are no sooner arranged than they are abandoned in turn for others appearing more feasible." It was as though an important component of Gage's ability to plan ahead rationally had been removed along with part of his brain.

The theory of behavioral economics is that if we could grasp a better knowledge of the brain, this might allow us to understand economics decision-making. As humans, we experience many cognitive and emotional stressors and when we do, we do not always act rationally, according to Standard Economic Theory. Furthermore, with all the increased stress or for no reason we can consciously identify, we can all agree that we make decisions that we later regret.

Scientific studies have shown that the route for the fear response in the brain bypasses the higher brain functions, including the ones we usually associate with rationality. Essentially, we fear things for reasons outside our conscious mind and we do this because we have no choice; we are physiologically hardwired to do so. It's as if we have our cognitive computer software (behaving, thinking, reaching conclusions, and making decisions) turned on with the emotional brain always running in the background.

So where does this all take place?

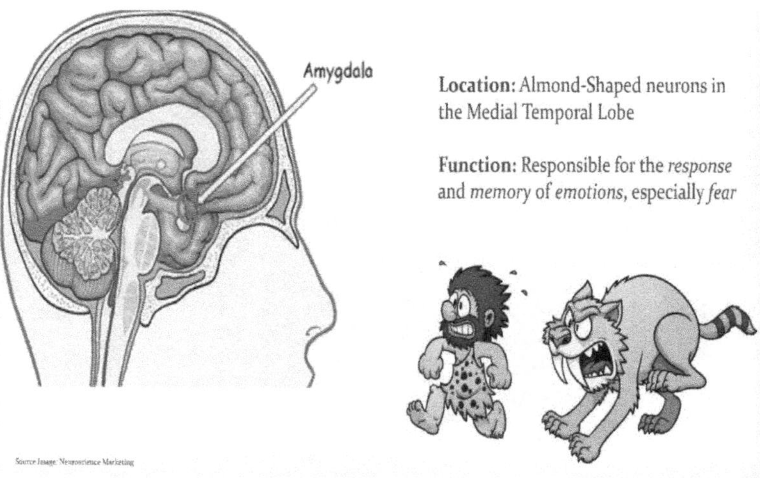

The amygdala. A small structure located deep within the brain, essential for *linking* memories to fear. In addition, the amygdala has direct connections to the brainstem, which is the central switchboard for all the muscles in our body. This neural shortcut—from fear to physical movement—is what allowed us in the early days of humanity, not to get eaten by a saber-toothed tiger.

Good thing for us that those days are gone, but the mechanism remains, hard-wired into our brains. The amygdala is the reason we are afraid of things outside our control, and it controls the way we react to certain *stimuli* or events that cause an emotion that is potentially threatening or dangerous—*whether real or perceived to be real.*

Knowing this, is there a way to turn it off?

Yes, but... Studies have shown that people with lesions or brain damage to this area behave more like theoretical machines. For example, an experiment in 1937 attempted to discover which areas of the brain were involved in the visual hallucinations caused by mescaline, the active chemical compound in peyote cactus. In the experiment, the researchers removed the temporal lobes of the lateral cerebral cortex of Rhesus Monkeys.

The monkeys' ability to see was not impaired, but their ability to recognize objects was. "The hungry animal, if confronted with a variety of objects, will, for example, indiscriminately pick up a comb, a sunflower seed, a screw, a stick, a piece of apple, a live snake, a piece of banana, and a live rat. Each object is transferred to the mouth and then discarded if not edible." At the same time, the monkeys also lost their sense of fear, behaving calmly in the presence of humans and snakes. The researchers had removed the part of the brain essential for linking memories to fear: the amygdala.

By understanding the characteristics and functions of the brain, the hundreds of cognitive biases, heuristics (or mental shortcuts—more on that later), combined with the data provided by DALBAR's three-decade study and my personal laboratory, I built this simplistic visual model called, "The Anatomy of Investor Returns" to depict the process we experience with each stimulus directed at the investor every day.

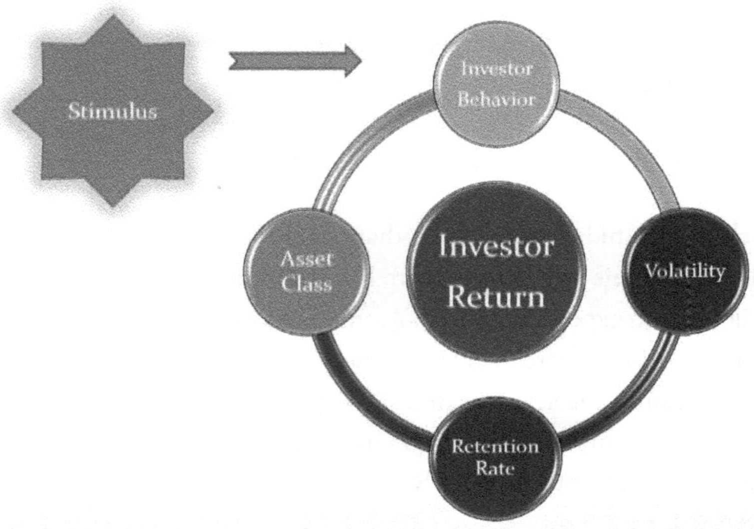

Although, we are no longer running from saber-toothed tigers, the stimulus we are running from, *financially*, elicits the same physiological responses. In other words, when it comes to financial decisions, we act like knuckle dragging cave people.

Let's examine some of its components:

One major financial *stimulus* is Wall Street strategists; they are famous for their prognostications, even though they have struggled with their accuracy:

Source: Barron's. From 1999 through 2005, numbers reflect Dow Jones Industrial Average forecasts. In 2006, Barron's began using the S&P 500 Index exclusively.
Past performance is not a guarantee of future results.

The chart shows that although they are never shy to prognosticate about where the market will be over the next year (shown as a smooth light grey line), the actual returns of the market just do not seem to follow those same predictions (shown as the random dark grey line). I do not fault them or believe these "experts" are unintelligent individuals (they're much smarter than me). However, they are paid by their firms to give opinions to the clients they represent (larger institutions, pension funds, and such), although it is a losing battle. Why? Nobody knows where the markets will be in the short run. Nobody. Well, at least those who are willing to tell the truth.

Unfortunately, the public is mesmerized by what will happen in the future—and predicting financial markets isn't much different than the industries of fortune telling or the live psychic lines. Let's face it, we would all love to know the unknown, but the reality is it *is* unknowable.

In fact, Harvard Economist, John Galbraith, after a lifetime of studying his craft, concluded that, "The only function of economic forecasting is to make astrology look respectable."

Sources: Federal Reserve Bank of Philadelphia & Department of Commerce. Concept Courtesy: James Montier

Again, the chart above shows the average forecast of economist prognostications of the growth rate for the economy in the near future or Gross Domestic Product (GDP). However, the actual GDP does not seem to want to follow those same predictions.

For those yearning these types of forecasts from their brokerage firms, understand this simple truth: the economy is normally uncorrelated to the markets over any short-term timeframe. Even if you had some secret knowledge of what the economy was going to do next, you would still have *no clue* as to what the markets' performance would reveal.

For example: At the bottom of the Great Recession in 2009, if you would have been asked how the economy was going to perform over the next four years and by some freak of nature, you knew the answer, you would have most likely said something to the effect, "Over the next four years, we will have the slowest economic recovery, *ever*. GDP will grow between 1% and 2%, and unemployment would never get under 7%."

And based on that sparkling outlook, as an investor, you would have done what?

Most likely kept your investments in a money market fund for the next four years—which most investors did—while the equity markets went up 140%. When the market bottomed on March 9, 2009, the "official" end of the recession was not called until the following February of 2010 by the president. Again, markets had already risen over sixty percent.

Now my favorite stimulus—The Untreated Financial Media Sewage—who rarely allow historical facts to get in the way of a good headline for clickbait:

Dow Jones second-quarter start is the worst since the GREAT DEPRESSION

Stock Market Pain Bleeds Into Junk Bonds

Stock market roller coaster

China imposes tariffs on American goods, sends stock market plunging

Chaotic Week for the Stock Market

Rattled Stock Bulls Cling to Predicted Earnings Surge

Dow Plunges In Worst One-Day Drop Ever

Source: Davis Advisors.

Financially speaking, these are the saber-toothed tigers.

How do we behave to these modern threats?

When discussing investor behavior, it is helpful to first understand the specific thoughts that lead to poor decision-making. Investor behavior is not just buying and selling at the wrong time, as DALBAR mentions. Investor behavior is also characterized by the psychological traps, events, and misconceptions that cause investors to act irrationally. And that irrationality leads to buying and selling at the wrong time, which leads to underperformance.

In addition, as Farnum Street Media states regarding behavior patterns and bias, stress causes both mental and physiological responses and tends to amplify the other biases. Almost all human mental biases become worse in the face of stress as the body goes into a fight-or-flight response, relying purely on instinct without the emergency brake of reasoning. Stress causes hasty decisions, immediacy, and a fallback to habit, thus giving rise to the elite soldiers' motto: "In the thick of battle, you will not rise to the level of your expectations, but fall to the level of your training."

DALBAR has found 9 distinct behaviors (cognitive biases) that tend to plague investors, though the degree of influence is based on their personal experiences and unique personalities. Let us examine a handful.

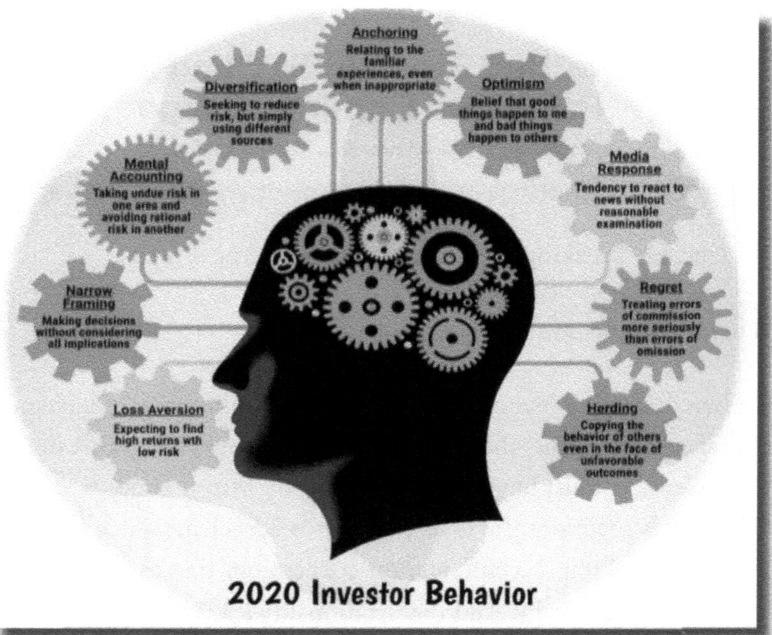

Loss Aversion:

> Behavioral science has proven that humans feel the pain of loss two times more than the pleasure of a gain. As Daniel Kahneman realized in test after test, "Many of the options we face in life are mixed. There is a risk of loss and an opportunity for gain and we must decide whether to accept the gamble or reject it…for most people, the fear of losing $100 is more intense than the hope of gaining $150. The conclusion is that losses loom larger than gains and that people are loss adverse."

You can test yourself on your level of loss aversion: What is the smallest level of gain you require to balance out an equal chance to lose $100. Behavioral Science found that to most people, the amount was $200, which is twice as much as the loss.

Mental Accounting:

We subconsciously categorize how money is earned and spent into different mental buckets that can get us in trouble. For example, have you ever taken a trip to Las Vegas? Most who have, before arriving, mentally set aside a dollar figure that they will be willing to spend and lose (let's just say few win). In addition, when a person wins money in Las Vegas, that money gets mentally set aside in your brain. However, it does not go into the same mental account as the money you earn from your job, which is usually set up to pay bills and live.

The money that has been "won" will be placed in a type of "play money" bucket that normally allows you to spend it with little care—with the mind easily justifying why it was spent (or wasted) on the third 68-inch flat screen. By the way, do not think for a moment that the casinos are not aware of *every* heuristic. Their job as businesses is to exploit them.

Anchoring:

We lock in prices for an item that all future decisions are then anchored to, all explained from a story about goslings (baby geese).

Dan Ariely, professor and author, serves as a James B. Duke Professor of psychology and behavioral economics at Duke University. In his book, *Predictably Irrational: The Hidden Forces that Shape our Decisions*, he explains how this bias works from an experiment.

It goes like this. A few decades ago, the naturalist Konrad Lorenz who won a Nobel Prize in Physiology in 1973, discovered that goslings (baby geese) became attached to the first moving object they encountered, which is normally their mother. He noticed that in the experiment, the goslings became attached and followed their mothers throughout their youth, by making initial decisions based on what they saw and sticking to the decisions once made.

In one experiment, Lorenz removed multiple eggs from a goose's nest. When the eggs hatched, he was the "parent" they saw, while the other geese from the remaining eggs knew only their biological parent. The fascinating aspect of this was Lorenz's goslings followed him around as if it were completely natural, and when he mixed the geese up, they would re-route themselves back to their identified "parents." He called this imprinting.

However, in humans, scientists call this anchoring. How, you may ask, does this relate to human behavior? Let me continue with the description from Dr. Ariel. He states that we are bombarded in life by prices, including suggested manufacturer's retail prices (for purchases like cars), lawnmowers, local housing prices of new or used homes. He states that these are not necessarily anchors to begin but *they become anchors* in our minds once we contemplate purchasing one of those items. This is when the anchor (imprint) sets itself into our mind and the decision-making process, as our mind subconsciously refers to the original anchor. Presto...you are now a gosling.

Regret:

Daniel Kahneman and Amos Tversky have described regret as the pain we feel when we easily imagine a different choice that would have led to a better outcome (remember Harry Markowitz). In real life, people make decisions to limit the feeling of regret, which is why rebalancing can be a difficult task. The emotional concern of, "*What if* I would have just let my winners run and would have more money in the portfolio?" Meaning, you may regret it if the stocks/funds continue to go up after you sold or reduced the amount in them to rebalance your portfolio. Even though, in the long run, this has been proven to increase an investors' returns (as seen later in the chapter on value of an advisor).

Herding:

When uncertain about what to do, we look to others for direction. We witness this heuristic (mental shortcut) in just about everything we do. For example, have you ever been driving on the highway during a new construction project? The orange barrels are guiding you to re-route into the oncoming traffic lane and you are not sure if this is the direction you should go, but everyone in front of you is doing it. So, what do you do? You follow the herd of cars.

When it comes to investing, like the animal kingdom, human behavior is somewhat primitive, as seen in the photograph below of the inside zebra. We instinctually feel more comfortable inside a group or herd during uncertain times, whether it be euphoric market tops or panic bottoms.

The alternative to going out on your own or doing what does not follow the rest of the public may be getting eaten by the lions, like the outside zebra. At least that is what you FEAR will happen, and in the financial markets, those fears are reinforced by the financial media.

Speaking of fear, is there a way we can measure it in investors? Yes. It is called the VIX or Volatility Index. How does this work? How does it relate to the markets? Technically speaking, the VIX (per Investopedia) was created by the Chicago Board Options Exchange (CBOE), as a real-time market index that represents the market's expectation of 30-day forward-looking volatility. Derived from the price inputs of the S&P 500 index options, it provides a measure of market risk and investors' sentiments.

It is also known by other names like "Fear Gauge" or "Fear Index." Investors, research analysts, and portfolio managers look to VIX values as a way to measure market risk, fear, and stress before they make investment decisions.

What are we looking at here? The bottom graph (labeled Volatility) will show the "spikes" from the year 2010-2020 as an event or crisis shocks investors' emotions. In addition, the name of the event/crisis is summarized. That event will correlate directly to the chart setting at the top of the VIX, defined by the S&P 500 Index.

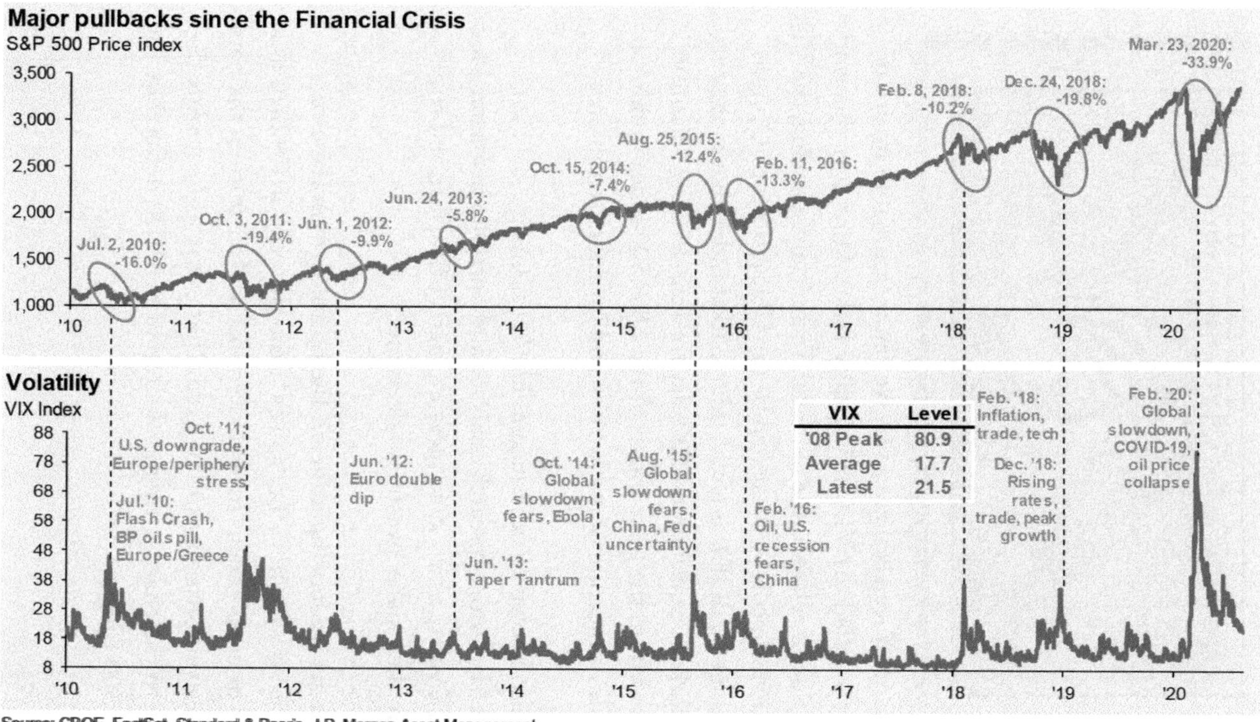

Source: CBOE, FactSet, Standard & Poor's, J.P. Morgan Asset Management.
Drawdowns are calculated as the prior peak to the lowest point.
Guide to the Markets – U.S. Data are as of August 18, 2020.

What you are witnessing is fear or panic in real time for each event and how it affects the market. As we've described in the Anatomy of Investor Returns diagram, the stimulus we have just discussed has now triggered our *investor behavior*. For example, you can see the drop (pullback) in the market by percentages during one of these occurrences since the Financial Crisis. In particular, the most recent is during the COVID-19 pandemic. The VIX spiked to a high of close to 88 (bottom of graph) and if you follow the results of that spike, the fear from the investors' pulled the market down by 33.9% (top of graph). Hence, stimulus and behavior.

What do most investors call these types of pullbacks in the market?

Go ahead, say it. *Risk.* We are now witnessing another misconception hidden deep in the suitcase. This one may not want to come out because it is so packed into the suitcase it has almost become part of the leather itself. The full misconception is embedded as confusing *risk with volatility*.

If we look back into our discussion on planning and how we have defined money as purchasing power, you should have now realized that the real risk is defined as outliving your money. Volatility, which we have witnessed in the VIX charts, simply reflects the daily/monthly/yearly ups and downs that the market *has and always will experience*. Common as dirt. And understand that volatility goes in both directions—up and down.

We love to say it is volatile when the markets temporarily drop but nobody wants to admit (because they like this type) that when the markets go up dramatically, that still reflects volatility. You cannot pick and choose your terminology based on your emotions attached to either the enjoyment or pain. Volatility is Volatility is Volatility. But what it's NOT is risk, unless you have chosen to redefine it that way in your brain.

Why so deep a discussion on this issue?

Because it is the crucial determinant of why investors behave themselves out of the long-term returns that they deserve (The Investor Gap in the prior chart). Solution? Reprogram your mindset to view it as a welcomed event in the permanent ups, historically, that the markets have provided.

By wishing away the daily volatility that the equity markets provide, you are wishing away the one thing that will get your family's long-term wealth to and through retirement.

Embrace it.

So how do these jolts in fear (VIX) relate to the market's yearly returns? When you read the section on Bear Markets and Corrections, you will understand.

A final reinforcing concept on risk, as we define it, will hopefully be grasped by these simple charts which I have gone through in prospective client meetings:

Drawing a simple chart on a legal pad with a vertical line showing Risk and a horizontal line showing Time, like below.

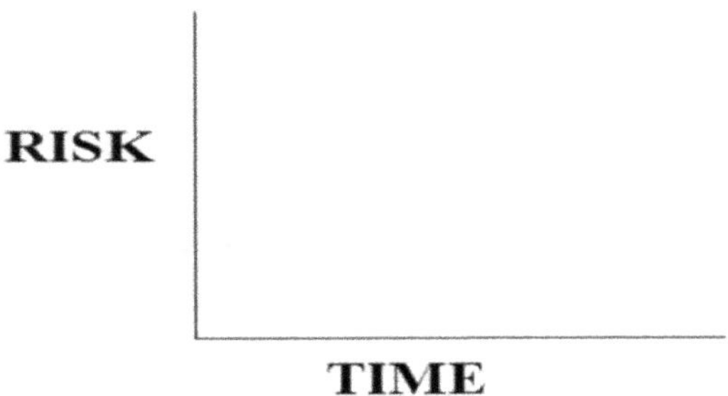

In the short run, your principal risk of being invested in equities is high. For example, in 2020 alone the market dropped drastically in a few weeks with the onset of COVID-19. We can see this on the chart by placing a bold arrow high up on the vertical risk side. But over time, based on the facts and history of the markets over any 30-year period, the risk to principal has been virtually ZERO, shown by the line going down over time (per the chart from Professor Seigel since 1802).

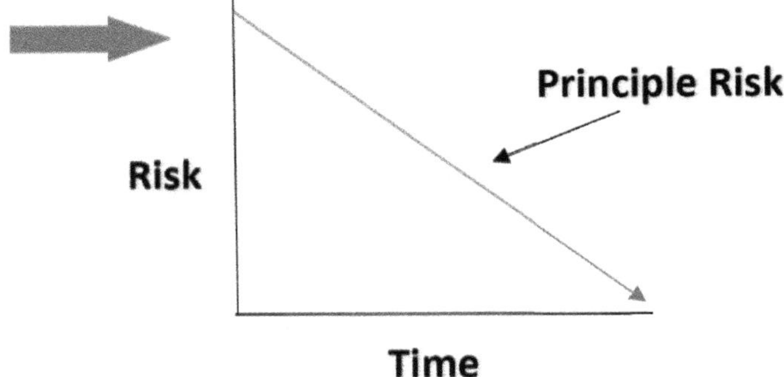

On the other hand, in the short run, your purchasing power risk—what you buy every day to survive—is the exact opposite. It would be rare that you went into the grocery store on any given day and the price of a can of tuna went up by 60%. Therefore, over time—as seen by the postage stamps—your purchasing power/cost of living will rise.

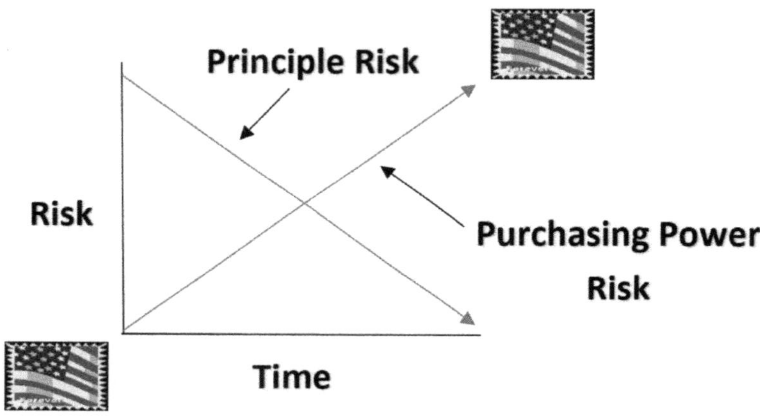

What happens to most retirees is that they begin retirement knowing at that time they need a specified amount to live on. Naturally, in the short run, they feel SAFE because by placing too much into fixed income assets, the volatility is low. But they are essentially SAFELY GOING BROKE over time because their fixed income does not continue to rise as the cost of living does. This is why the bucket system works.

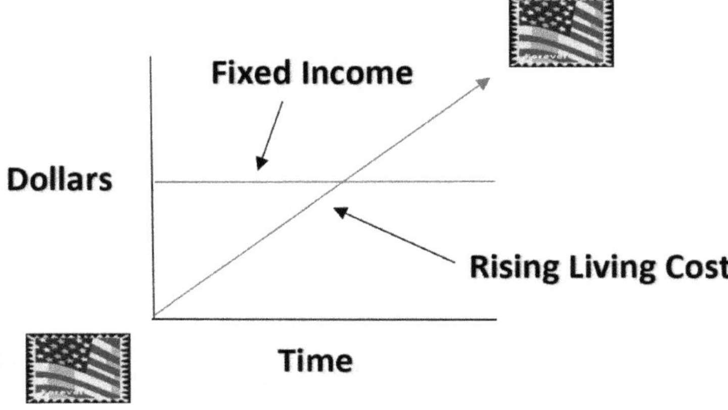

Charts – Source: Nick Murray. Based on a concept outlined in Nick Murray's book entitled "Behavior Investment Counseling."

The next discussion in our Anatomy of Investor Returns is *Retention*, as illustrated in the chart below.

As the chart indicates, over the past 20 years, equity mutual fund investors have seldom managed to stay invested for more than 4 years. When they have done so, it has been during periods of bull markets. Which reminds me of a quote from Warren Buffett, "The stock market is a device to transfer money from the impatient to the patient."

Retention Rates: Equity Funds

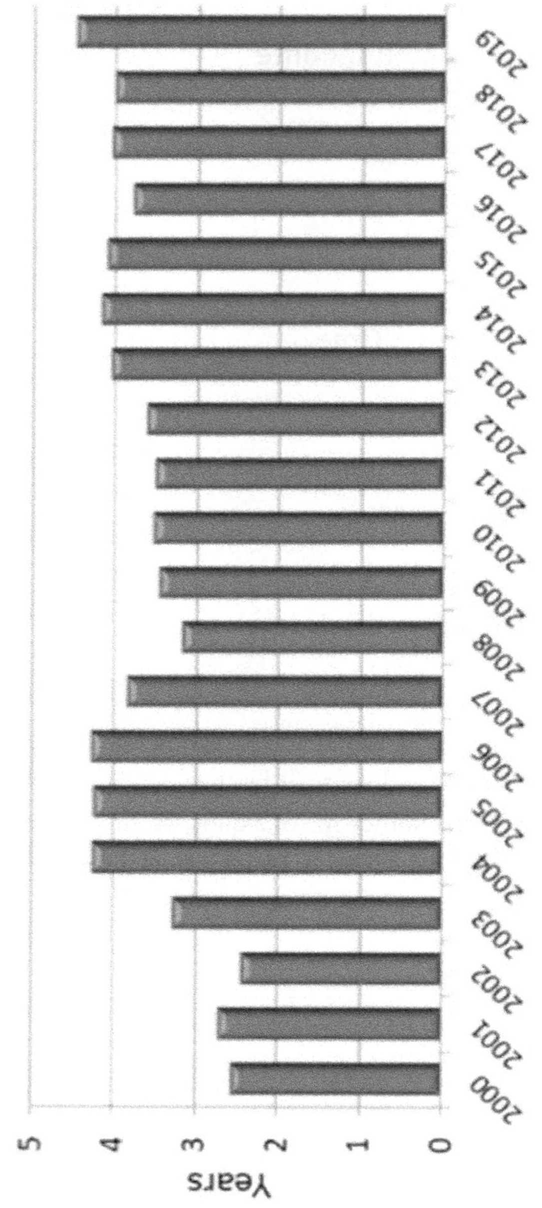

Source: "Quantitative Analysis of Investor Behavior, 2020," DALBAR Inc. www.dalbar.com

The data in the graph shows that the average mutual fund investor lacks the *patience* to stay invested for a long enough period to execute a long-term strategy. Typically, it is for just a fraction of a market cycle. For example, in 2017, the market conditions caused an expected effect on retention rates—an increase in all areas, due to low volatility. This was different from 2016, when the retention rates plummeted as the elections were underway, which increased volatility and uncertainty. What tends to happen is that investors withdraw funds when markets decline or there is a fear of a crisis—*real or perceived*. The effect of the increased withdrawals reduces retention rates and the ability to capture the long-term returns of the funds/ETF the average investor is in.

The final category in the Anatomy of Investor Return is *Asset Class Return*.

Although I touched on this point in the section about the portfolio, it is a good refresher to remember that the long-term return of each asset class is historically tied to the level of volatility it endures, as described below.

Money Market/Checking and Savings: How much volatility do these have? None. And they should not, because you need those dollars to pay bills and short-term costs. As a result, how high of a return do you receive on those dollars invested in this assets class? As expected, the answer is *almost zero*.

Bonds: What type of volatility do bonds exhibit? Higher than money markets but usually nowhere near the daily swings that stocks provide. As a result, what has been the historical return of this asset class? They have earned *around 3.5% after inflation*.

Stocks: Their volatility? In the short term, massive amounts of volatility can happen with much higher swings than both bonds and cash. As a result, what has been the historical return on this asset class? Historically, stocks have gained *around 6.8% after inflation.*

What have we learned? There is a direct correlation between an asset class's volatility and its historical long-term return. And there is an inverse relationship between certainty and return. The more uncertainty an investor can stomach, the higher that investor's long-term return has been, historically. Simply stated, if you want a higher return you must embrace uncertainty.

In summary, the anatomy of an investor's behavior is as follows:

Some outside stimulus triggers your unconscious behavior, which leads to fear and panic selling and thus increases the overall volatility in the markets. Due to the increased uncertainty (volatility), investors begin to sell their most volatile investments and leap into bonds or cash. When the herd piles their portfolio into the bonds or cash, their long-term return will be reduced based on the historically low level of return—after inflation—these assets classes have provided since 1802.

We are now confirming the data that DALBAR has provided over the last thirty years: the average investor has behaved themselves out of close to 50% per year. Once again, sad, but true as history shows us.

****

Special COVID-19 Analysis:

We have witnessed, during the COVID-19 pandemic, some extreme swings in volatility with the markets on a daily basis. Let's examine how the average investor has been actually reacting based on the DALBAR data in real life.

The Average Equity Fund Investor Retention Rates chart shows that over the last year, retention rates reached a historical low in March of 2020.

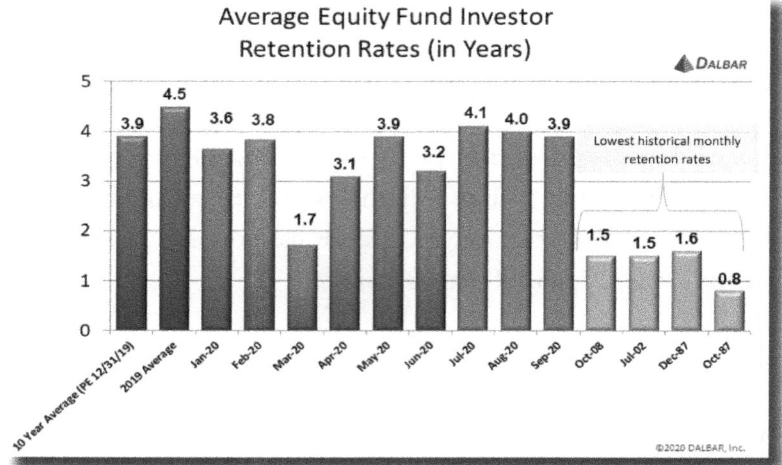

What you are witnessing from the chart above are the following facts provided by DALBAR:

As a reminder, retention rates measure cash outflows in proportion to assets to arrive at the length of time the average investor holds a fund, if the current redemption rate persists.

- After reaching an annual average of 4.5 years in 2019, retention rates hit historical lows of 1.7 years in March.
- The only month that has registered a significantly lower retention rate than March of 2020 was October of 1987, when retention rates hit an all-time low of 0.8 years.
- In April, retention rates stabilized while still remaining low in terms of its recent averages.
- In May, retention rates reached their 10-year average before dipping back to lower levels again in June.
- In the third quarter, retention rates remained at or

slightly above their 10-year average but still short of their levels in 2019.

According to DALBAR, this suggests the following:

The Average Equity Fund Investor did not alter their contribution/ withdrawal pattern with respect to equities until the 3rd quarter. However, the average equity fund investor was still busy moving money during the plunge in March, as the velocity of money movement skyrocketed. This suggests that the Average Investor was busy changing investment selection while not necessarily reducing equity exposure.

The next question we would need to ask, after reviewing the findings from above is how did the moving of money from one asset class to the next do versus our "Winnie the Pooh" recommendation earlier of just doing nothing?

The graphs below examine the Hypothetical $100,000 Equity Portfolio. The first is the Average Equity Fund Investor and the second is the Average Buy and Hold strategy, which would earn the rate of return of that of the S&P 500 Index (and represents the non-emotional approach).

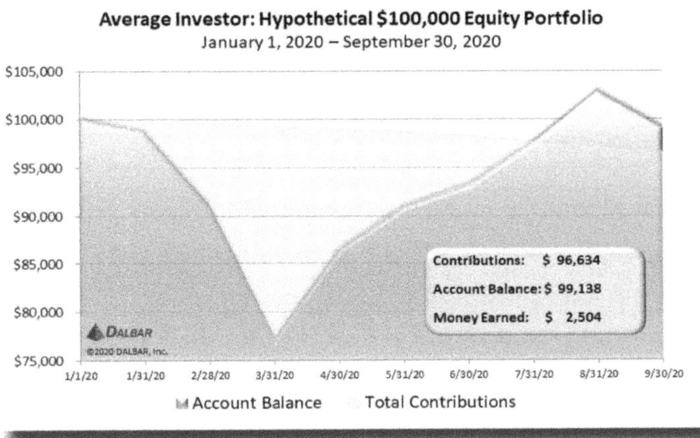

The Average Equity Fund Investor with a hypothetical $100,000 equity portfolio withdrew $3,366 in the first 9 months of 2020, while gaining $2,504. This left the Average Equity Fund Investor with an ending balance of $99,138.

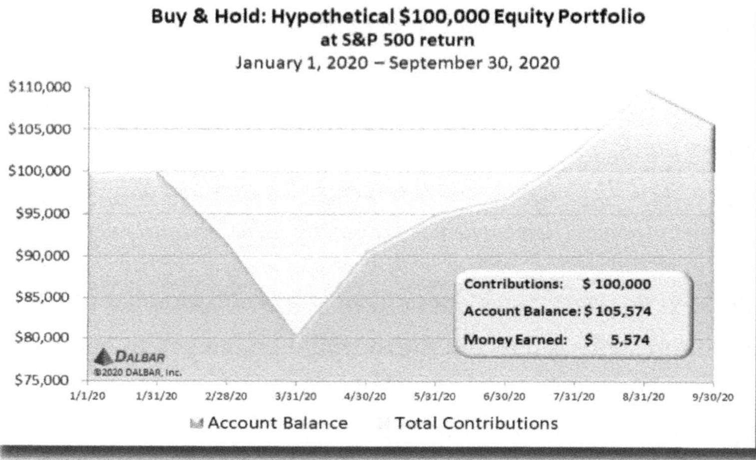

A hypothetical buy and hold strategy of $100,000 earning the return of the S&P 500 over the first 9 months of 2020 would have yielded an account balance of $105,574; a gain of $5,574.

Results? Winnie the Pooh wins…again.

The final analysis to come from DALBAR in their "Investor Insights: COVID-19 and Financial Advice," DALBAR, Inc. (www.dalbar.com) is summarized below:

In August of 2020, they surveyed over 995 investors in North America who have a relationship with a financial advisor. The respondents were presented with various questions about their experiences with investing, the markets, and their advisor during COVID-19. Although the majority of investors were satisfied with the advice given to them by said advisor (over 80% in most cases), there was one finding that struck me as interesting.

Why do I say interesting?

Given the facts from the above charts of the hypothetical equity portfolio, comparing what investors did (how they reacted) vs. a buy and hold (Winnie the Pooh, do nothing) approach, we know the buy and hold was *the* way to go. Again, my mantra: "If your goals haven't changed, don't change your portfolio."

However, the beast in the suitcase reared its ugly head once again—as human nature always will.

Let me quote the LEAST satisfactory advice given, "Investors who followed their advisor's recommendation to *do nothing* reported the lowest satisfaction in their advisor." Go ahead, read it again. Welcome to my world. Sometimes giving the advice the clients *need* is not always what they *want* to hear. Which brings us back to the reality of the original investor behavior chart at the beginning of the chapter. The investor behavior penalty or gap of 9.96% vs. 5.04% per year for 30 years. These are the defining moments which can determine your family's long-term wealth.

Chapter Takeaways:

- The psychology that drives investors is always essentially the same. Investor behavior is triggered by some form of stimulus—either a geo-political event, previous market experience, news stories, or a tip from a colleague/family member that distracts investors from their long-term goal.

- Since 1994, DALBAR (an independent research firm) reveals its Quantitative Analysis of Investor Behavior (QAIB) that measures the effects of investor decisions to buy, sell, and switch into and out of mutual funds over short and long-term timeframes, revealing that doing nothing yields the best returns.

- The Investor Behavioral Penalty means that on average, when investors make emotional decisions, they gain less than they would have if they had just done nothing. For the thirty-year period ending in 2019, these are the returns as follows: S&P 500 at 9.96% per year vs. Average Equity Investor (with emotions) of 5.04% per year.

- The dominant determinant of long-term, real-life investment returns is the behavior of the investor.

- The amygdala is a small structure located deep within the brain, and its function is the part of the brain essential for ***linking*** memories to fear. The amygdala is the reason we are afraid of things outside our control, and it controls the way we react to certain *stimuli* or an event that causes an emotion that is potentially threatening or dangerous—*whether real or perceived to be real.*

- By wishing away the daily volatility that the equity markets provide, you are wishing away the one thing that will get your family's long-term wealth to and through retirement. Embrace it.

- The Anatomy of Investor Return show that Stimulus → Investor Behavior → Volatility → Retention Rate → Asset Class → Investor Return
  - Some outside stimulus (Wall Street Strategists, Economists, and Financial Media) triggers your unconscious behavior, which then increases the overall volatility in the markets. Due to the increased uncertainty (volatility), investors begin to sell their most volatile investments and leap into bonds or cash. When the herd piles their portfolio into bonds or cash, their long-term return will be reduced based on the historically lower level of return—after inflation—these assets classes have provided since 1802.

Bear Markets and Corrections

A market downturn doesn't bother us.
It is an opportunity to increase our ownership of
great companies with great management at good prices.

– Warren Buffett, Chairman, Berkshire Hathaway

Many individuals have taken some sort of trip on a cruise ship in their lifetime. However, for those of you who have not (or a refresher for those that have), do you remember what is the first thing that happens just before you get ready to leave port?

Envision this: you get on the ship and are looking around, with the excitement of an upcoming relaxing vacation. After finally getting all your things stored into your cabin, maybe you have been able to sneak a pre-launch beverage of choice or even a casual stroll to the gaming area or pool deck.

Just as you are settling into a comfortable chair on the deck, you hear the captain say, "Would all passengers please return to their cabins to get your life jacket and proceed to the upper levels for a lifeboat drill." You're probably thinking, "Wait a second; we've just left port and we're sinking already? What ship did I get on, the Titanic (as you check the name on the side of the ship once again)?"

No, in fact, every cruise line that leaves port must review the safety procedures (lifeboat drill) just in case the ship does begin to sink. Will it sink? Probably not, but as a passenger you need to be prepared for the rare occurrence, lest you become part of Davey Jones' Locker.

Essentially, the drill is intended to stop those passengers from panicking and jumping overboard when the vessel encounters rough seas. In addition, they have a set of procedures or plan of emergency in that rare event the rough seas become an "iceberg" event. Wouldn't it be nice if we could have the same lifeboat drill for the financial markets? How about calling it the Financial Lifeboat Drill?

For example, the chart of the S&P 500 Index below will show you a history of "rough financial seas." These are called, from Wall Street's view, *bear markets*.

BEAR MARKET CHRONICLES

Dates of Market Peak	Dates of Market Trough	% Return	Duration	Market Peak	Market Trough
05/29/46	06/13/49	-29.5%	36.5 Months	19.3	13.6
08/02/56	10/22/57	-21.5%	14.5 Months	49.7	39.0
12/12/61	06/26/62	-28.0%	6.5 Months	72.6	52.3
02/09/66	10/07/66	-22.2%	8 Months	94.1	73.2
11/29/68	05/26/70	-36.0%	18 Months	108.4	69.3
01/11/73	10/03/74	-48.0%	20.5 Months	120.2	62.3
09/21/76	03/06/78	-19.4%	17.5 Months	107.8	86.9
11/28/80	08/12/82	-27.0%	20.5 Months	140.5	102.4
08/25/87	12/04/87	-33.5%	3.5 Months	336.8	223.9
07/16/90	10/11/90	-20.0%	3 Months	369.0	295.5
07/17/98	08/31/98	-19.3%	1.5 Months	1186.8	957.3
03/24/00	10/09/02	-49.2%	30.5 Months	1527.5	776.7
10/09/07	03/09/09	-57.0%	17 Months	1565.1	676.5
04/29/11	10/03/11	-19.4%	5 Months	1363.6	1099.2
09/20/18	12/24/18	-19.8%	3 Months	2930.8	2351.1
02/19/20	03/23/20	-33.9%	1 Month	3386.1	2237.4
AVERAGE		**-30%**	**13 Months**		

Before we dive into the events themselves, let's make sure everyone understands just what a bear market is. They are defined by a drop in the market's peak (top) to trough (bottom) by 20% at closing. In full disclosure, you will notice that I have added four (4) events in the chart that have "technically" not quite closed down twenty percent. In turn, the financial media and market technicians will dismiss these claims—my response is that you just need to ask anyone with an adult memory how it *felt*. Understood? I will hold that my chart's depictions reflect those emotions of investors.

Now that you understand what a bear market is, why do they occur?

The answer is simple: normal business cycles or unforeseen events. First, the business cycle. Without having to get too technical, as if you are taking a business economics course in college, the economy (and the businesses that comprise it) is always weaving through expansions and contractions, meaning times are slow, then pick up, get much better, and finally begin to be excessive (euphoria). Once they reach that peak, they inevitably drop (contract) into a trough.

However, as human nature intervenes, these normal ups and downs in the business cycle get pushed to extremes with investor emotions. As the chart below shows, emotions don't always match what is actually happening in the market.

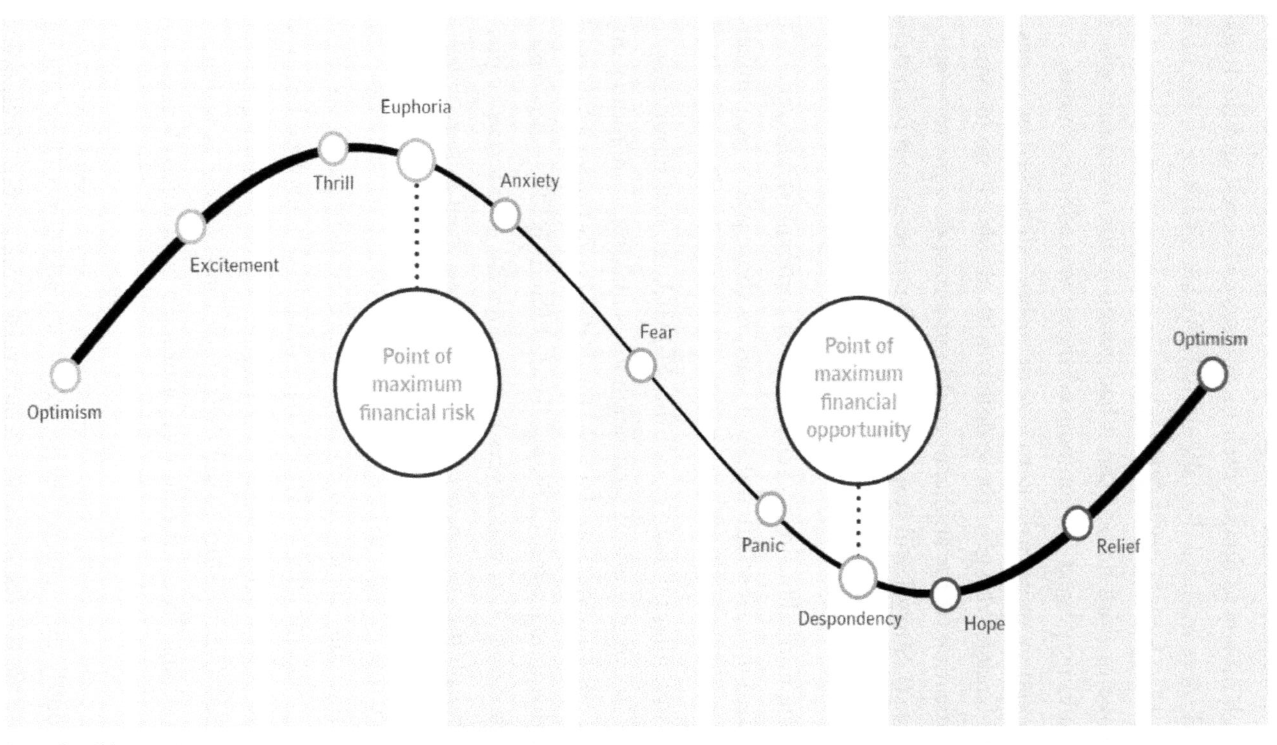

Source: Russell Investments.

For example, in expansionary times, people begin to borrow too much money to finance their businesses or homes, and the banks lend more to those they should not. We are all aware of the housing crisis back in 2007-2009 when everyone seemed to have a second or third home. And it had gotten to the point that when a building project just announced that it was adding condos, speculators went rushing to give deposits—all backed by banks and lenders who gave those dollars with absolutely no income verification (if the applicant could put a mist on a mirror—approved). Sorry, I will stop here as we do not want to rehash those painful memories.

In the normal business cycle, prices of company stocks get pushed up to levels that do not warrant those prices (remember the dot.com era), as the euphoria of making money overwhelms the investing public. We call this FOMO, the fear of missing out. In other words, if your neighbor is making more money on that "thermo-nuclear dot.com fund" than your boring high-quality dividend paying Exchange Traded Fund (ETF) —now you missed out. As it will always be, the emotion of *investors* begins to morph into *speculators* and finally reveals itself as pure *greed*.

Once this reckoning hits, as the normal business cycle begins to contract, businesses can no longer pay their debt payments, housing payments stop, and bank loans default. All involved begin to panic, which will cause banks to tighten up on providing capital (loans) and investors to sell their stock funds in fear of losing everything. This is the human nature of a business cycle, shot to its extremes. It happens time and time again.

Secondly, unforeseen events can pull a market into a bear market. These are the rogue waves on our cruise ship, as they catch everyone by surprise. As the old saying goes, "Surprise is the mother of panic." To name a few, the terrorist attacks on 9/11 and the COVID-19 virus/pandemic of 2020 were such events. The common characteristic in these events is the enormous level of fear of the unknown that grips the world and investors. Understandable, but in the long-term it is irrational—as it pertains to the market's reactions and inevitable pullback.

Why do I say this?

Think of it this way, the value of a business is rarely tied to its day-to-day stock price because a business's value does not change much quarter by quarter—as most stock analysts portrays. The stock price is a projection of what the company's values (or earnings projections) could be over the next twelve months, which is still somewhat unknowable. Any business owner will tell you that projects get delayed, cancelled, and added.

It is a continuous cycle, contrary to stock analysts' expectations for stock prices in the short-term. If this is still somewhat confusing, think of it in comparison to your home value. Can you imagine a "home analyst" providing you a projection on the value of your house every quarter or daily? And adjusting it by the new carpet, bed sheets or paint color that you decided to add or held off on purchasing?

The simple fact is this—the longer-term price of a business (or businesses that make up the stock market index) will follow one primary factor. Earnings. Where earnings go, prices will follow. Sometimes they are disconnected temporarily but again we are focusing on the longer-term view.

What are the other concepts one need understand about bear markets?

Hopefully, the chart reveals their utter commonness. There have been ***sixteen*** bear market since the end of WWII. This will average out to about ***one every five years*** with an average drop of about ***30%*** —and they last about ***thirteen months***.

Stop and read this last statement of facts again. And again.

If you work for about 40 years, you will encounter about eight and when you retire over a 30-year period, you get to enjoy around another six. As nicely as I can, I'll sum up these historical facts—they are as common as waking up in the morning, so get used to it, if you endeavor to be an equity investor.

The beacon in the harbor (since we are on this theme) for all we have learned about bear markets should be this historical fact—***all bear market drops are temporary, and the advances are permanent.***

Go ahead, look at the chart again. Go on. I'll wait for you here because these are vital concepts every investor must emotionally grasp. Okay, you're back. As you can see, during the first bear market in May of 1946, the S&P 500 peaked at 19.3. As I write these words today towards the end of November 2020, the S&P 500 is at 3629.

Each one of those fierce growling bears brought about utter fear and capitulation for the majority of investors who went through them. And to add salt to the wound, each event the financial media spewed its message of how it was "the-end-of-life-on-the-planet-as-we-know-it." However, the index is around 190 times higher than it was from the first peak, and we have not even added dividends to this return. But why make it look any prettier...you get my point.

What can be learned from this chart is simple:

1. Since the end of World War II, we have had 16 of these potentially capsizing financial waves hit us as investors (our industry refers to them as Bear Markets).
2. These average out to be about one every five years with the average drop of around 30%, with the duration being about 13 months.
3. *So far, each new market peak is above the prior market trough—that means we did not sink.*
4. Every crisis above we have had thrown at us, we have been able to survive and thrive. As Chris Davis of Davis Advisors has said, "Crises are a painful but inevitable part of the investing landscape."
5. Since the market peak of our first event in 1946, the market has gone up over 190 times (not including dividends) as of November of 2020.
6. *While the ups and downs of the market move in cycles, the declines (market troughs) have not eclipsed the advances (market peaks). Which brings us to our historical conclusion:* ***All declines have been temporary, and all advances have been permanent.***

Hopefully, this will allow you to enjoy your life-long investing cruise and give you some perspective if you are thinking about jumping out of your investment portfolio when the next wave hits.

Market Corrections

The time to repair the roof is when the sun is shining.

–John F. Kennedy, U.S. President, 1961-1963

I have always been amused (yes, a bit of twisted humor) by the financial media's obsession over the words, *market correction*. And how they will race to interview all those market strategists from the Wall Street firms who are going to "predict" the next market correction.

Picture this scene: the financial wizard in the thousand-dollar suit will pause as the question is asked by the talking head, then begin to ponder for a moment, as if really trying to determine something...genius. Then the wizard says with confidence, "Blah-blah-blah (a time over the next few years)." Da-da-dum. The talking head commentator says, "Wow! Really?" as if the secrets of life have just been revealed for the first time on earth.

The reason I poke fun at these conversations is what has been revealed in the chart below on market corrections, since 1980. The chart illustrates that even when there has been an average intra-year drop of almost 14%, in most years the annual returns on investment have been positive. An intra-year drop is defined as the difference between the peak and the trough during a single calendar year.

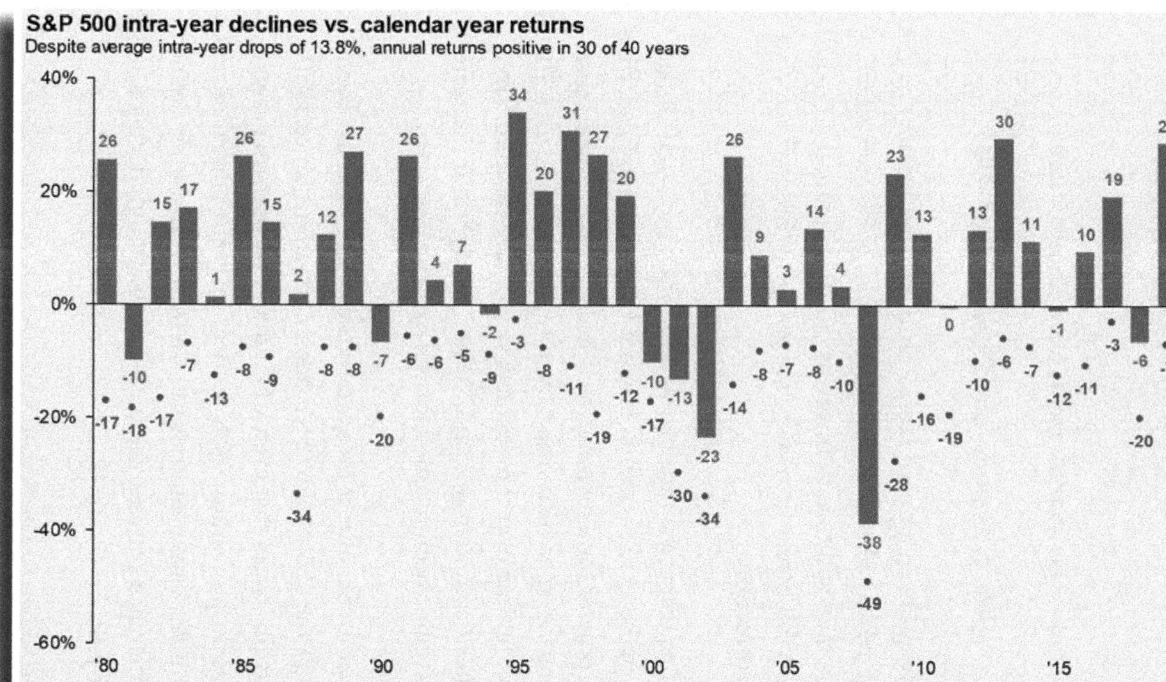
S&P 500 intra-year declines vs. calendar year returns
Despite average intra-year drops of 13.8%, annual returns positive in 30 of 40 years
40%
20%
0%
-20%
-40%
-60%
'80
'85
'90
'95
'00
'05
'10
'15
'20
YTD
5
Source: FactSet, Standard & Poor's, J.P. Morgan Asset Management.
Returns are based on price index only and do not include dividends. Intra-year drops refers to the largest market drops from a peak to a trough during the year. For illustrative purposes only. Returns shown are calendar year returns from 1980 to 2019, over which time period the average annual return was 8.9%.

Furthermore, what you are seeing is each year's return from January to December in grey. For example, in 1980 the market was up 26% for the calendar year. However, at some point between January and December of that same year in 1980, the market was off from its peak (-17%) as shown below the current year bar. We call this the intra-year decline versus the calendar year return. Again, even though the market was positive (26%) for the year, at some point during that same year, it had a temporary dip of 17%.

The reality of market corrections is this: since 1980 the market has experienced an intra-year drop that averages 13.8% per year. Again, the key fact to remember is that these drops have historically been temporary. However, despite the temporary dips each and every year, the market has been positive 30 of those 40 years or 75% of the time. Which circles back to my amusement of the experts' predictions and how the media clamors over forecasting when these elusive events will occur. Ah, how about this answer: on average, the market has dipped about 13.8% per year since 1980—not rocket science—but has recovered even more. Turn the channel.

Market Bubbles/Manias

People start being interested in something because it's going up, not because they understand it. But the guy next door, who they know is dumber than they are, is getting rich, and they aren't.

– Warren Buffett

In the book, *Manias, Panics, and Crashes: A History of Financial Crises* (third edition), author Charles P. Kindleberger explains how the typical pattern (historically) of a mania turns into a bubble, this way:

> There is nothing so disturbing to one's well-being and judgement as to see a friend get rich. When the number of firms and households indulging in these practices grows large, bringing in segments of the population that are normally aloof from such ventures, speculation for profit leads away from normal, rational behavior to what has been described as "manias" or "bubbles." The word mania emphasizes the irrationality; bubble foreshadows the bursting.

Although the financial media indulges in the giddy pleasures of wordsmithing the most terrifying and alluring scenarios to catch the momentary emotional glimpse from the average investor, in the previous century, we can say that we've witnessed only about three. Now, some advisors might argue for different numbers based on varying definitions; however, using the definition from above and the quote from Mr. Buffett, I would timestamp those three events as:

1. 1927-1929 (the roaring twenties)
2. 1965-1968 (the go-go era)
3. 1997-2000 (the internet/dot.com era)

Now that we understand how they occur and when they have taken place—what is the best strategy for the average investor's portfolio and long-term financial plan? We need to revisit some of those practices discussed earlier in the book—two in particular—diversification and rebalancing. Go ahead, I'll wait here while you refresh yourself on those concepts in the chapter on The Practices.

In addition to these practices, the earlier conversation with the *SC Carrier* about our philosophy encapsulates the advisor's primary role—to not allow the client to get caught up in the euphoria in the first place.

It is vital to have a fact-driven conversation to counterbalance the financial media's blissful potion of don't-miss-out, live-for-today directed at investors daily. Let's just say that it may be easier to herd a barnyard full of cats. Nevertheless, in order to avoid the destruction of a lifetime of planning, the experienced advisor must act as a behavioral coach and must prevail.

Having experienced one of only three of these in the past one hundred years, the primary driver and solution (in my opinion) was to redirect the clients' focus to their financial plan. Maybe it had the sobering effect of reality or just served as a momentary diversion away from all the glitter. I am not quite certain which it was, but I do know this—it worked.

The Value of Advice

Maybe you're wondering if you need an advisor...in my experience, the best financial advisors can add extraordinary value...for me, getting first-rate advice has been a game changer. I'm a capable guy and pride myself on understanding the most important principles... but I'm not about to do brain surgery on myself.

– *Tony Robbins, Motivational Speaker and Author,* Unshakable: Your Financial Freedom Playbook

It is a question that has been and will be asked by clients or prospective clients: Are you worth your fee? This may not have been verbalized, but do not believe for a moment you were not thinking it. Every. Time. You. Meet. Your. Advisor. Understanding this justifiable concern, how does the advice giver demonstrate to the client/prospective client their value?

If you are a Registered Investment Advisory (RIA) Firm or CERTIFIED FINANCIAL PLANNER™ practitioner, it can be somewhat of a challenge. It is even a greater hurdle if you are a broker/investment advisor (defined below). Why? You cannot guarantee investment performance—nobody can. And the falsely driven belief perpetuated by the financial media is that outperformance of investments is *the* sole purpose most investors should engage the advice giver.

Research from an independent source says that financial advisors are worth their fee—specifically if they do these activities below. And as a certified financial planner (CFP®) for eighteen of my twenty-five years in this industry, I have found that most do not. Sad. But true. But for those who do, the data from the study reveals an enormous value.

Russell Investments provided an annual report titled 2020 Value of An Advisor Study, "which looks holistically at the real, measurable value advisors deliver for their clients, in their portfolios, and in vital services advisors provide. We developed a formula to calculate the full value equation of an advisor's services."

The formula and services analyzed were as follows:

A = **Annual** rebalancing of portfolio

+

B = **Behavioral** mistakes individual investors typically make

+

C = **Cost** of basic investment-only management

+

P = **Planning** cost and ancillary services

+

T = **Tax-Smart** planning and investing

Once the cost of the services is added up, they are compared to the average annual advisory fee in the industry, which is typically around 1% per year of the assets the advisor is managing for the client. The formula created was meant to quantify (as most of what an advisor provides are intangibles) both the technical and emotional contributions provided by an advisor. The services analyzed and percent gain are discussed below.

Annual Rebalancing: *+0.32%*

One may not believe that rebalancing provides a difference in the lifetime return of the average investor; however, anyone with an adult memory who recalls the peak of the dot.com bubble knows it most certainly did. In its simplest form, a properly diversified portfolio is built to match the investor's most cherished long-term goals, based on the client's plan and the historical market returns of each asset class.

As the chart below reveals, a hypothetical balanced index portfolio in January of 2009, if the allocation was based on the client's financial plan and then never touched (rebalanced), will have morphed into a much different blend ten years later in 2019. In this scenario, equities have increased 21% and fixed assets have decreased 18%. Unintentionally, the portfolio, left to the ebbs and flows of the market, has evolved from a typical growth-and-income mix to growth-dominated portfolio. Not a bad allocation, if this was the intent, but most likely it was not.

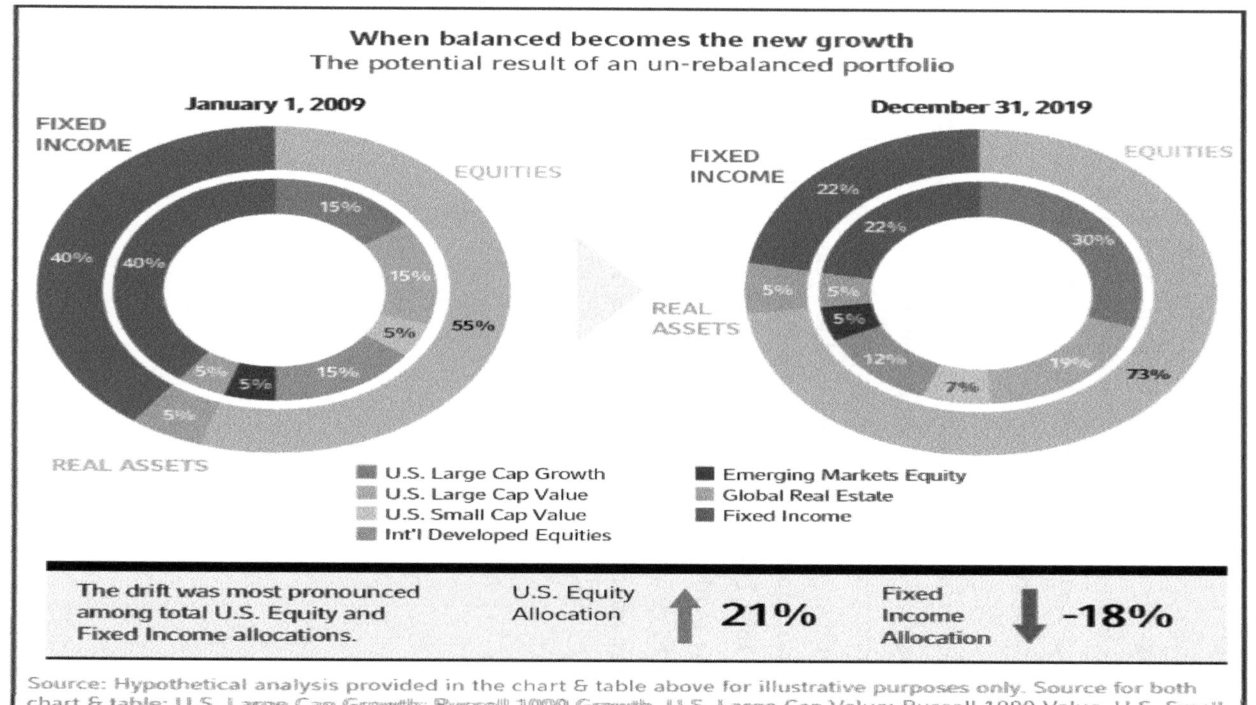
When balanced becomes the new growth
The potential result of an un-rebalanced portfolio
January 1, 2009
FIXED INCOME
EQUITIES
REAL ASSETS
40%
40%
15%
15%
5%
15%
5%
5%
5%
55%
December 31, 2019
FIXED INCOME
EQUITIES
REAL ASSETS
22%
22%
30%
5%
5%
5%
12%
7%
19%
73%
U.S. Large Cap Growth
U.S. Large Cap Value
U.S. Small Cap Value
Int'l Developed Equities
Emerging Markets Equity
Global Real Estate
Fixed Income
The drift was most pronounced among total U.S. Equity and Fixed Income allocations.
U.S. Equity Allocation
21%
Fixed Income Allocation
-18%
Source: Hypothetical analysis provided in the chart & table above for illustrative purposes only. Source for both chart & table: U.S. Large Cap Growth: Russell 1000 Growth, U.S. Large Cap Value: Russell 1000 Value, U.S. Small Cap: Russell 2000, International Developed Equities: MSCI World ex USA, Emerging Markets Equity: MSCI EM, Global Real Estate: FTSE EPRA NAREIT Developed, and Fixed Income: Bloomberg Barclays U.S. Aggregate Bond.

To further illustrate, the actual dollar figure that rebalancing added annually to the client's long-term goals from March of 2005 to December 2019 is depicted in the chart below:

Hypothetical rebalancing comparison of $500,000[1]
March 2005–December 2019

		BUY AND HOLD	ANNUAL REBALANCING
0.32% =	**Annualized return**	6.73%	**7.05%**
	Standard deviation	9.3%	**8.9%**
	Ending value	$1.3 million	**$1.4 million**
	Reduction in portfolio volatility		↓ **-0.4%**

[1]For illustrative purposes only. Not meant to represent any actual investment.

Standard deviation is a statistical measure of the degree to which an individual value in a probability distribution tends to vary from the mean of the distribution. The greater the degree of dispersion, the greater the risk. See disclosure details on methodology and criteria.

Source Portfolio: Diversified portfolio consists of 30% U.S. large cap, 5% U.S. small cap, 15% non-U.S. developed, 5% emerging markets, 5% REITs, and 40% fixed income. Returns are based on the following indices: U.S. large cap = Russell 1000® Index; U.S. small cap = Russell 2000® Index; non-U.S. developed = MSCI EAFE Index; emerging markets = MSCI Emerging Markets Index; REITS = FTSE EPRA/NAREIT Developed Index; and fixed income = Bloomberg Barclays U.S. Aggregate Bond Index. Start date corresponds to index start dates (January 1988 is the inception of the MSCI Emerging Markets Index).

Although it may not seem to be a large percentage increase (0.32%), when applied to a portfolio beginning at half a million dollars rebalancing results in growth to $1.4 million rather than $1.3 million without rebalancing. In this case, $100,000 is a nice difference in additional gain for the client. All accomplished by just rebalancing once per year. The next question may be, "*When* should the rebalancing take place?" Simple. As close to the same day each year as possible. Why the same day? Because anything other than this and the advisor/client become a "closet market timer."

Why wouldn't every investor do this? Annual rebalancing is countercultural to how the average performance junkie behaves—buy high (or adds to what is going up) and sell low. Rebalancing forces the portfolio, which is a servant to the client's plan, to sell what has just shot the lights out and add the proceeds to what has been in the doghouse. And cognitively/behaviorally, it is not an easy thing to accomplish. Hence, it is countercultural.

Behavioral mistakes: *+2.17%*

As mentioned earlier, human nature is a failed investor. Our prehistoric brain, proven by studies in behavioral science, is hardwired with cognitive bias and heuristics that lead the average investor to *react* to market events as a perceived threat (shown below as the monthly inflow and outflow of money from Mutual Funds/ETFs). This behavior is no different than how the caveman would *react* to the threat of a saber-toothed tiger at full charge, fangs protruding.

As the chart below depicts, from January 2000 to December 2019, $100 constantly invested in the Russell 3000® Index more than tripled in value to $350 (the solid line). By the way, those that chose to stay in cash during that period missed a cumulative return of nearly 250%, based on the Russell 3000® Index (so an investment of $10,000 would have become $25,000).

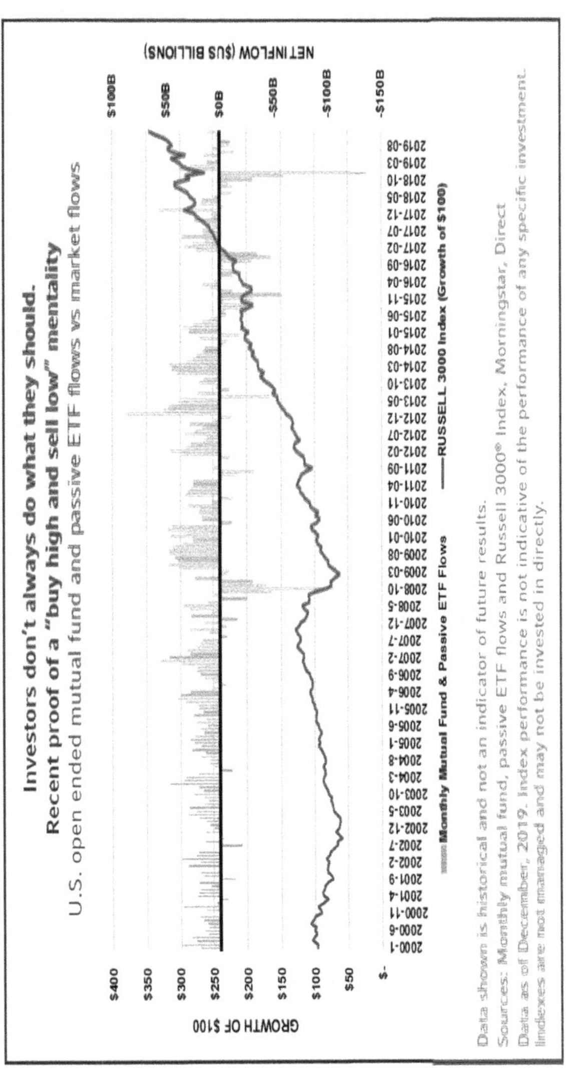

Before we can venture any further, let me briefly explain a concept that has been growing in popularity—in just about every field—it is called behavioral finance. To fully grasps this concept, we need to first understand what it has evolved out of — Standard Finance or Economic Theory.

Without getting too complex, it can be summarized with the following story: an economist is strolling down the street with a friend and they come up to a $100 bill laying on the ground. As the friend reaches down to pick it up, the economist says, "Don't bother. If it were a genuine $100 bill, someone would have already picked it up."

The point of the story isn't to ponder whether they were the first to come upon the bill or not, but rather to illustrate that the economist believes all people are rational.

As Richard H. Thaler explains in his book, *Misbehaving: The Making of Behavioral Economics*. "The core premise of economic theory is that people choose by optimizing. All the goods and services a family can buy, the family chooses the best one it can afford...make choices that assume to be unbiased...we choose on what is called rational expectations."

Again, it is built on four foundational blocks:

1. People are rational
2. Markets are efficient
3. People should design portfolios based on Mean Variance Portfolio Theory
4. Expected returns for investments are defined only by risk

Conversely, in an interview in June 2005 from *The Monitor* titled, "What is Behavioral Finance?" Meir Statman, PhD, says, "Behavioral finance is a framework that augments some of the parts of standard finance and replaces other parts." Primarily, he is stating that investors are "normal" not rational. Investors are not stupid, but it's understood that we are human and have cognitive biases that need to be overcome.

You have seen a similar chart from the chapter titled, The Anatomy of Investor Return, showing how the average investor behaved themselves out of close to 50% of the returns they deserved from the period of 1988 to 2019, when compared to the S & P 500 Index. I felt it was worth reinforcing and providing a much broader index to compare (so those in our industry would not feel I was "cherry picking" an index or time frame), in addition to expanding the years of comparison by another four years. The investor behavior gap shown from Russell Investment research below as the comparison of the Average Investor vs. the Passive Russell 3000 Index:

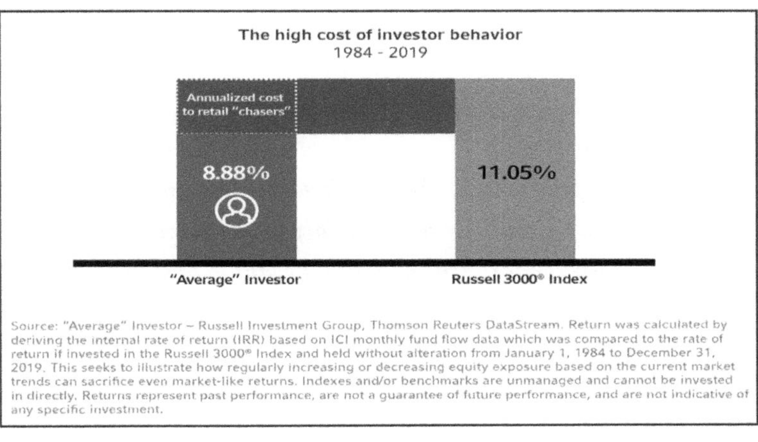

Source: "Average" Investor – Russell Investment Group, Thomson Reuters DataStream. Return was calculated by deriving the internal rate of return (IRR) based on ICI monthly fund flow data which was compared to the rate of return if invested in the Russell 3000® Index and held without alteration from January 1, 1984 to December 31, 2019. This seeks to illustrate how regularly increasing or decreasing equity exposure based on the current market trends can sacrifice even market-like returns. Indexes and/or benchmarks are unmanaged and cannot be invested in directly. Returns represent past performance, are not a guarantee of future performance, and are not indicative of any specific investment.

Once again, discussed in the chapter on behavior and worth the refresher and reinforcement (as we know that repetition is the mother of skill), behavioral finance tells us we have over 200 different cognitive biases (aren't we lucky?). The most common to investors pitfalls are again summarized as the following:

- Loss Aversion

  We value gains and losses differently. We feel the pain of loss twice as much as the pleasure of a gain.

- Overconfidence

  A tendency to hold a false and misleading assessment of our skills, intellect, or talent. In short, it is an egotistical belief that we're better than we actually are.

- Herding

  Going with the crowd. Assuming things are good or bad because others are doing the same.

- Mental Accounting

  Although every dollar is the same, we mentally attach a different value on each dollar, based on how it was acquired.

- Familiarity

  the preference of the individuals to remain confined to what is familiar to them. They wish to remain within their comfort zone and do not want to take the path never taken.

Cost of investment-only management: +0.29%

The next obvious question asked is, "What would the cost be for a robo-advisor?" According to Russell Investment, robo-advisors that deliver investment-only management and no financial plan, ongoing service, or guidance have set prices at approximately 0.29%—for annual statements, online access, and a phone number to call in case of questions. The chart below depicts what will be provided to those who choose to use the robo-advisor services—asset allocation, security selection and portfolio construction.

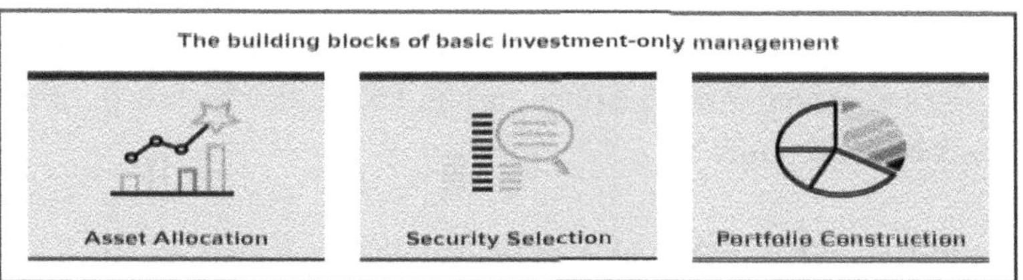

Based on the average fee charged for investment-only management by 10 robo-advice offerings for a client portfolio of $500,000 as accessed on Ignites Article = Top 10 robo-advisors June 2018, bankrate.com/investing/best-robo-advisers/, and individual robo advisor websites on 2/6/2020.

Planning: *+0.72%*

The foundation of any successful planner/client relationship is a comprehensive financial plan. Let me state this simple but powerful fact one more time: *it is the foundation.* Anything less is smoke-and-mirrors wrapped in a bow of the asset management package—or some may argue, an Investment Policy Statement (IPS). An IPS is essentially a stripped-down version of a comprehensive financial plan for those who are not interested in anything other than investment advice from an advisor. Being the self-proclaimed voice of reality, I would say that if asset allocation and investment selection are all the advisor is providing, the client is most likely better off at a robo-advisor.

The asset allocator may have been sufficient in the years prior to the 1990s, but not anymore. How can one be certain of the prior statement? There is NO historical evidence for the persistence of performance. None. So, planning is *the way* to financial freedom—hence the process overseen by The Certified Financial Planning Board Code of Ethics and Standards of Conduct.

It's worth asking how much the financial planning component costs nowadays. Per a financial planning study conducted by financial planner Michael Kitces, the average standalone planning fee for a comprehensive plan was around $2,080, which is 0.52% on a $400k account.

In addition, what is the value of typical ancillary services an advisor and their team offer? The value of the ancillary services provided to clients includes addressing insurance needs, custom requests, and questions. These additional services can quickly consume 20, 50, or 100 hours each year. If the advisor is providing these ancillary services, Russell Investments estimate that the total planning fee goes up by an additional 0.20%.

Now adjusted, the average standalone planning fee for the most comprehensive plan with ancillary services was $2,880, which is 0.72% on a $400,000 account.

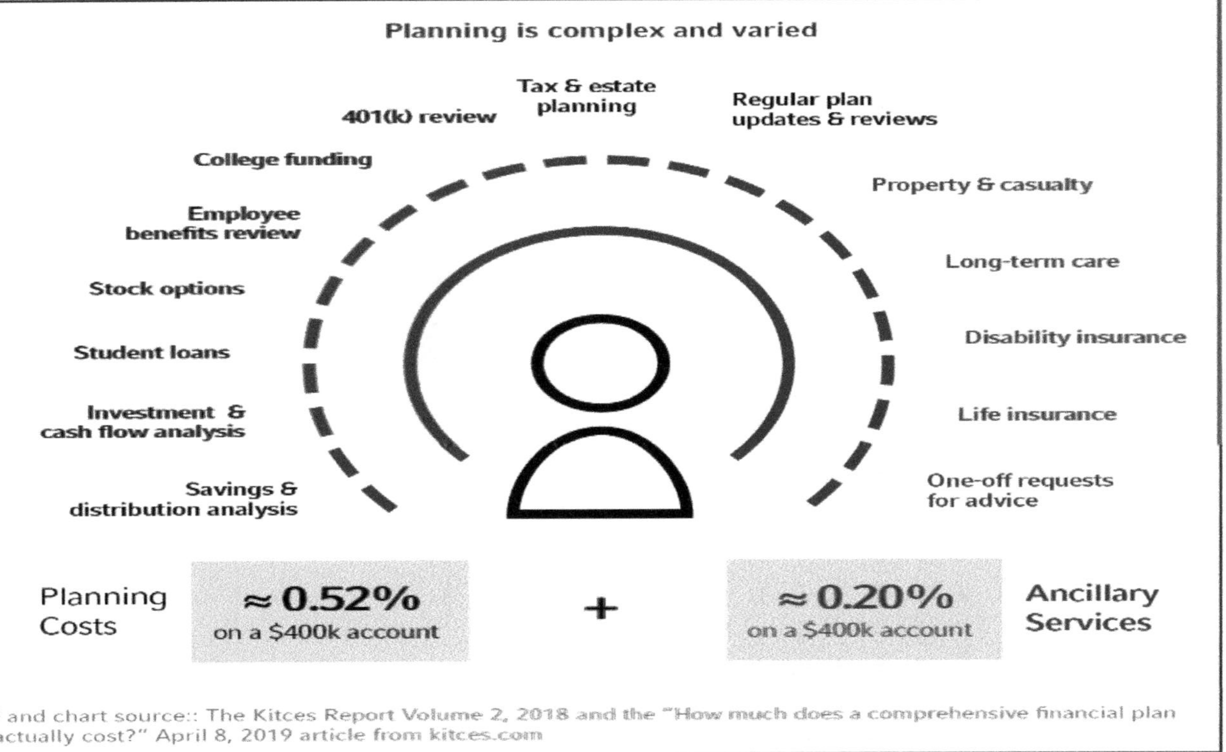

[2] and chart source:: The Kitces Report Volume 2, 2018 and the "How much does a comprehensive financial plan actually cost?" April 8, 2019 article from kitces.com

Tax-Smart Investing: *+1.31%*

How much return can be added with a tax-smart approach? According to Russell Investments, the average annual tax-drag for the five years ending December 31, 2019 was significant. As shown in the table below, investors in non-tax managed U.S. equity products (active, passive, and ETFs) lost on average 1.85% of their return to taxes. Those in tax-managed U.S. equity funds forfeited only 0.54%, that is a value difference of 1.31%. As an example, on the same $400,000 portfolio that we have shown above, it would equate to a $5,240 tax drag. With taxable investors holding $9.8 trillion of the $21.3 trillion invested in open-end mutual funds, this is a massive concern—and a massive opportunity for added value.

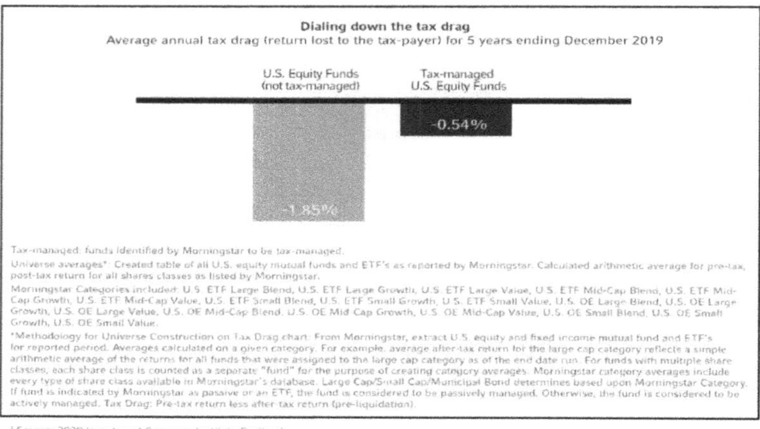

[2] Source: 2020 Investment Company Institute Factbook.

THE BOTTOM LINE: WHAT IS YOUR ADVISOR'S VALUE?

A = **Annual** rebalancing of portfolio
+ 0.32%

B = **Behavioral** mistakes individual investors typically make
+ 2.17%

C = **Cost** of basic investment-only Management
+ 0.29%

P = **Planning** cost and ancillary services
+ 0.72%

T = **Tax-Smart** planning and investing
+ 1.31%

TOTAL VALUE OF ADVISOR

4.81%

TYPICAL ADVISOR CHARGE FOR SERVICES

1%

The bottom line: If the provider of advice cannot provide multiples of the value of their annual fee, the client should (and is better off) go elsewhere. According to Russell Investments, the advisor can provide said value if he/she adheres to a comprehensive approach.

In full disclosure, Vanguard provided a similar study in 2014 titled, "Advisor Alpha." They believed that the total value an advisor provided was about 3% per year, broken down into the following categories:

- Portfolio Construction: 1.2%,
- Wealth Management: 1.05%
- Behavioral Coaching: 1.50%

Below is the overview of the study (source: Vanguard—Advisor Alpha March 2014):

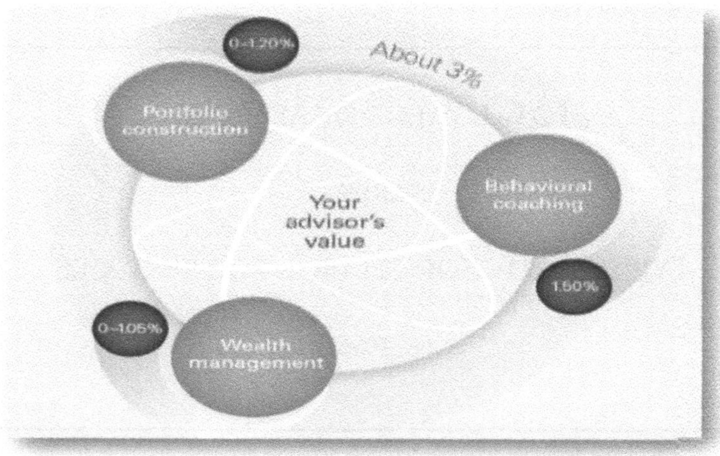

Quantifying your advisor's value	Potential value relative to "average" client experience (in percentage of net return)
Portfolio construction	
Suitable asset allocation using broadly diversified mutual funds/ETFs	>0%
Use of low-cost index-based products	.45%
Asset location between taxable and tax-advantaged accounts	0–.75%
Total-return versus income investing	>0%
Wealth management	
Regular rebalancing	.35%
Spending strategy for drawdowns	0–.70%
Behavioral coaching	
Advisor guidance to help adhere to financial plan	1.5%
Potential value added	"About 3%"

Source: Francis M. Kinniry Jr., Colleen M. Jaconetti, Michael A. DiJoseph, and Yan Zilbering, 2014. *Putting a value on your value: Quantifying Vanguard Advisor's Alpha.* Valley Forge, Pa.: The Vanguard Group.

Note: For "Potential value added," we did not sum the values because there can be interactions between the strategies.

Annuities

The Good, the Bad, and the Ugly

Full disclosure: I am not a big fan of annuities. However, understanding that they are an extremely popular product sold to retirees, I will provide the "facts" only. Once revealed—you can decide if it fits your planning needs. And, as the subtitle states (from the classic Clint Eastwood movie), you will get the good, the bad, and the ugly.

To begin, annuities have become an extremely complicated product to understand as they've continuously evolved. This complexity exists not only for the average investor (who I believe doesn't completely comprehend) but for the industry and advisors who sell the product.

The best way to sum it up, is by discussing the confusing mystery, espoused in the movie *JFK*. If you recall the scene where Jim Garrison (Kevin Costner) is questioning David Ferrie (Joe Pesci) in the hotel room about who shot President John F Kennedy:

Jim Garrison: And who killed the President?

David Ferrie: Oh man, why don't you *bleepin' stop it? This is too *bleepin' big for you, you know that? Who did the president, who killed Kennedy! It's a mystery! It's a mystery wrapped in a riddle inside an enigma! The *bleepin' shooters don't even know! Don't you get it?

Why are annuities so alluring? Because we all love a mystery—and we all love thinking we have solved it. Investors are also called by the siren song of the sales pitch (my opinion) which appeals to our natural human cognitive bias. Which bias? Loss Aversion. And the insurance industry has fine-tuned the message. You may be wondering what key words they use to sing the song. Just to name a few, they claim guaranteed income, guaranteed minimum return, no downside risk, and safety.

If you've grasped the concepts set forth in this book, you will begin to understand that these products appeal to real concerns of most retirees—outliving their money and an inherent fear of volatility (again, which most believe to be risk). One more concept that plays into the minds of the retiree, as I explained in the opening chapter of the book, is that the baby boomers have been forced to move away from Defined Benefit Plans (pensions) provided by their former companies. The future retiree has gone from, "taken care of" by the company to you are "on your own." The change can be utterly terrifying for most retirees who have not assembled a comprehensive financial plan.

So, there you have the cognitive reasons for the popularity of the annuity product. Now let's view the product itself and its structure.

What is an annuity?

An annuity is a contract, issued by an insurance company, which allows the owner to accumulate money tax-deferred for long-term financial goals and eventually receive income from the annuity as retirement arrives. When retirees are ready to receive income from the annuity, they can withdraw funds as needed, or set up a regular payment schedule for a given period—guaranteed by the issuer. However, withdrawals from annuities before age 59½ may be subject to ordinary income tax and a 10% tax penalty from the IRS.

There are essentially only three types of annuities:

1. Fixed Annuities
2. Variable Annuities
3. Indexed Annuities

A *fixed annuity* generally offers a guaranteed fixed or minimum interest rate for a stated timeframe. Depending on the terms of the contract, the insurance company may adjust the rate periodically. The contract owner makes a lump-sum payment or a series of payments and, at some point in the future, they receive the lump sum back or monthly lifetime payments, plus the stated interest rate.

There are two types of fixed annuities:

The first type is one in which the insurance company guarantees the interest rate for a specified timeframe, typically 5 to 6 years, with a principal return feature in the event the investment is liquidated prior to the specified holding period. At the end of the guarantee period, you may elect to continue, surrender the contract, or receive income in a variety of ways (annuitization).

The second type has a market value adjustment (MVA) feature which may result in a gain or loss in the contract if surrendered prior to the end of the rate guarantee period. Be sure you understand which type of fixed annuity you are purchasing before investing.

The final critical point to remember is that all guarantees are based on the claims paying ability of the issuing insurance company. Meaning, if they go out of business, all bets are off. So, the "guarantee" is no longer in existence—which brings up a valid point of making sure the insurance company offering the product is highly rated.

The Good: fixed rate, almost zero volatility as it acts almost like a Certificate of Deposit (CD) at the local bank and can provide a lifetime of income. Low fee structure.

The Bad: the rates are normally low and usually don't keep up with the cost of living (purchasing power). The contract may lock the purchaser into the annuity and charge an exit fee if the owner wants all the monies due to an unforeseen event.

The Ugly: once annuitized, the assets become part of the insurance company, and if there are financial issues, the guarantee is gone—unlike a bank CD that has FDIC insurance. Also, once annuitized, the payments of income stop upon the annuitant's death, unless a rider (the bells and whistles added at an extra cost) is purchased.

The second type of annuity is the *variable annuity*, which is comprised of two areas: investments and insurance. As the picture below shows, the annuity is wrapped up as part insurance and part investments in mutual funds.

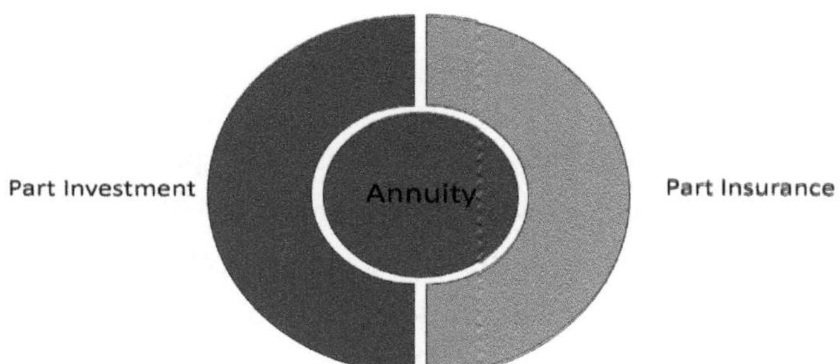

Designed to provide an income stream while protecting against longevity and market risks.

A variable annuity is primarily the insurance industry's way to get into the investment business and the trillions of dollars which are available for companies to manage and charge a fee. As shown in the diagram, the variable annuity is a wrapper of insurance around mutual funds—called sub-accounts.

There are usually two phases to the variable annuity called *the accumulation phase* and *the distribution phase*. The accumulation phase is simply the paying of premiums into the contract and choosing the sub-accounts either with a lump sum (called a premium payment) or continuous payments over time.

The distribution phase (payout phase) is when the monies are paid out to the contract owner, usually monthly. The rate of return provided by the contract is dependent on the returns of the sub-accounts (mutual funds) chosen. So, unlike the steady stream of payments that are attached to the fixed annuity, the variable annuity's payment stream will fluctuate based on the investments.

The solution the insurance provider has come up with are *riders* that can offer a guarantee minimum base amount of income—but for a price. Essentially, you're investing no differently than any other investment strategy, with one critical variable—additional insurance cost.

The Good: they not only provide added insurance protection (death benefit) but can provide a higher return to offset inflation when investment returns in the sub-accounts perform well. In addition, the funds will grow tax deferred until withdrawn after the age of 59 ½. And, unlike an IRA or 401(k) that grows tax deferred, there are larger limits to the amount you can add.

In addition, if this is the mental comfort needed in order for the investor to stay invested and not panic out of the returns they deserve when the markets become volatile, then something is better than nothing.

The Bad: they come with the following fees: Mortality and Expense, Administration, Sub-Account, and fees for any rider that is chosen. There is also no guarantee of the protection of principal loss since the monies are most likely invested in the markets. All gains taken are not taxed at the lower capital gain rate but ordinary income rate, as if it were a paycheck.

The Ugly: they have back-end fees and rider costs. These fees normally lock the contract owner into a time-frame of 7 to 15 years before they can access all their monies. If taken beforehand, penalties of up to 12% will be taken from the contract owners' account. In addition, all the "guarantees" that come with the advertised sales tactics are normally built into the riders that can add up to as much as 4.24% annually (according to the SEC research).

One way to analyze the value of investing in a variable annuity is to look at the average long-term returns since 1926 of large company stocks, which has been around 10%. If you give away up to 4.24% per year, or more than half to fees, that is quite an uphill battle just to break even. If viewed from this perspective, you could invest in the same Large Company Stock Index and keep the 4.24% in your "non-variable annuity" account.

The most common question is, "Why do I have to pay the back-end fees to lock up the money?"

Most commonly, the commission paid to the broker or insurance agent can range between 5% to 7% up front of the premium you paid. As a business, the insurance company needs time to recoup those commissions paid—hence the lockup period.

The reality of owning this with all the "bells and whistles" of up to 4.24% is that you are paying a high annual fee for *perceived certainty*. And as an added benefit, your money gets to stay in jail—locked up by the back-end fees (there I go showing my bias).

The final type of annuity, developed most recently, is *Indexed Annuities*. These are the most confusing to comprehend. In full disclosure, the last contract I read (more likely, deciphered) took me hours to read and I still had to map it out on a piece of paper to understand. Then I called the insurance provider, who offered the product, and it took two different employees before *they* understood what it meant. No Joke. This was not for a product I was recommending, but from a new client that it was sold to by a prior insurance/advisor and I had to figure out how it worked.

The indexed annuity combines the features of both the fixed annuity and the variable annuity, which means they try to provide a minimum guarantee return with a potential upside based on (linked to) an equity index—like the S&P 500.

The terminology they like to use is "market-like returns" with downside protection. At face value, it sounds like everything an investor would want to experience during retirement—when the market goes up, you get those returns and when it goes down, you're protected from those losses. However, with most products that sound too good to be true, it's always the details which must be understood.

The key terms you must understand are *participation rates and caps.*

So, what are these and how do they work? Although each has its unique definitions, in general these will explain how much the contract owner will get when the "market's up." For example, if the market index your contract is tied to goes up 10%, you don't get all of that increase. You will "participate or get capped" at let's say 50% of the return. So, the actual rate you received is half or just 5% of the return that year—before any fees assessed (which are usually hidden).

You may say, "Why would the insurance company do such a thing?" One reason is they need to bank those additional returns for a bad year to make up for the downside protection they are supposed to provide. So, when the markets go down in a given year, you're able to receive a minimum return (usually around 0-1%) and the portfolio does not turn negative. This is the terminology of "downside protection."

The Good: potential higher returns and downside protection.

The Bad: the complexity of gobbledygook of how each works.

The Ugly: participation rates and cap rates. The "smoke and mirrors" can be extremely misleading to contract holders. The sales pitches given are confusing to potential investors and the back-end fees to get out, once discovered, are expensive.

In addition to the tax-deferred earnings feature of annuities, there are other important tax issues to consider.

The first is the initial payment/premium paid to a Non-Qualified Annuity (meaning in a taxable account), known as the cost basis in the contract. Since it is usually previously taxed, the cost basis will not be taxed on withdrawal. For contracts purchased after August 14, 1982, a withdrawal must come from earnings first for tax purposes and any amounts in excess of cost basis will be taxed at your ordinary income rate.

If you withdraw earnings from an annuity before age 59½, you may be subject to ordinary income tax and a 10% penalty tax. A non-qualified annuity is not subject to the IRS mandatory minimum distribution at age 72.

You may exchange an existing annuity contract for a new contract without any tax consequences. This is called a 1035 exchange. This 1035 exchange privilege does not apply when switching from an annuity to a life insurance contract. Also, be aware that surrender charges and other fees may apply. You should not sign any exchange form until you study all the options carefully, understand all fees involved, and are satisfied that the exchange is better than keeping your current policy.

Purchasing more than one annuity contract from the same insurance company in any calendar year results in serial annuities. All of the contracts will be combined and treated as one contract for tax purposes.

When purchasing an annuity in a tax-qualified account, such as an IRA, no additional tax benefit is received. In other words, the IRA or 401(k) already provides tax deferral, and you can't get it twice. You should consider the other benefits of the annuity when deciding whether to purchase an annuity for your qualified account.

Knowing all we have gone over, in my opinion, the annuity debate begins with the following questions:

1. Can a client build a similar portfolio with traditional investments?
2. Do clients erode the benefits over time with the higher costs associated with the variable annuity, which can run up to 5.64% a year?
3. Would annuities be as popular for the advisors/agents in the industry to sell if they didn't pay so well—a commission of up to 7% of the investment made?
4. How about the ongoing advice from the person selling it? Once the advisor is paid, is there an incentive to continue to service the client?

These are all questions that you need to ask and understand.

And they should be thoroughly explained by the person offering the product, which is another issue to consider. As mentioned earlier, many people who sell these products don't understand the entire scope of what they are offering (frankly, they are somewhat confusing when new twists are added by the insurance companies each year). They are most likely told by their manager to "sell this product," and are given the bullet points of only the benefits without the drawbacks.

They may not know important information, such as what the effects of an annuity are regarding estate planning. There is no step-up in basis upon death. All gains come out as ordinary income instead of a possible lower long-term capital gains rate.

The bottom line is this: although the concept of an annuity has merit, the costs applied to every rider, which allows the benefit to be provided to the contract holder, defeats the purpose. Again, in full disclosure, in the twenty-five years I have been providing behavioral planning advice to clients, it only made sense in one case. Yes, just one. And the one I was able to provide to the client had no back-end fees, no upfront sales commission, and ongoing insurance costs of 0.30% per year.

Summary

All I want to know is where I am going to die, so I'll never go there.

-Charlie Munger, Vice Chair Berkshire Hathaway

The suitcase is empty. You have finally been relieved of the misperceptions that have been weighing on you and your family's long-term financial success, and—in hindsight—the reality was not a magic formula concocted by the financial media reflecting what they would have you believe it to be. It wasn't any hidden secret that any Wall Street firm, insurance company, or discount brokerage was peddling at the moment. This understanding brings to light the most important financial issues in life, viewed without the emotional brain entangled with human nature that we have been hard-wired to subconsciously battle. The financial issues are solved in a quote from the famed German mathematician Carl Gustov Jacob Jacobi. His theory was, "man muss immer umkehren" or freely translated as "invert, always invert."

Charlie Munger has explained, "Jacobi knew that it is in the nature of things that many hard problems are best solved when they are addressed backwards." To further explain, in his book *Worldly Wisdom*, Munger describes a time when he was to give a speech to the graduating class at Harvard University. As he began to pontificate how he decided on what to say that day, he said that he recalled a speech that was given by one famous celebrity, Johnny Carson, which he had wished would have been even longer. Johnny Carson's began with Carson's prescription for guaranteed misery in life. Why guaranteed misery? What

Carson said was that he couldn't tell the graduating class how to be happy but could tell them from his personal experiences how to guarantee misery.

Again invert, always invert.

My advice is to focus on your behavior. Or better yet, overcome the obstacles of human nature. I have discussed this concept multiple times throughout this book. In my position over the past twenty-five years, I have been fortunate (and unfortunate) enough to see just about every emotional response as it relates to people's money and family dynamics in the grips of challenging times. Just to name a few:

- 1997: Asian Financial Crisis / Mini Crash
- 1998: The Russian Financial Crises / Debt Default / Bear Market
- 2000: Dot-com Crash/ USS Cole Attacked
- 2001: September 11 Terrorist Attack, Enron Collapse
- 2002: Bear Market
- 2003: IRAQ War/ Space Shuttle Explodes/ SARS
- 2005: Hurricane Katrina and Rita
- 2006: Bird Flu
- 2007-2009: Great Recession and Financial/Housing Crisis
- 2008: Madoff Ponzi Scheme
- 2009: GM Bankruptcy / Swine Flu / Bear Market
- 2010: Flash Crash
- 2011: Bear Market
- 2012: Fiscal Cliff
- 2013: Boston Marathon Bombing
- 2014: Ebola

- 2015: Greek Debt Crisis
- 2016: Zika Virus / Brexit
- 2018: Bear Market
- 2020: COVID-19 Pandemic / Bear Market

What holds true to wealth, in both the creation and maintenance of a family's legacy, has always been its dominant determinant whittled down to the temperament of the individuals in these unknowable, inevitable events.

And through all these end-of-the-world-as-we-know-it challenges listed above, the S&P 500 has gone from 614 in December of 1995 (*when I began in the planning business*) to 3,629 as of November of 2020. That equates to about a bit higher than a 6-times increase. If we look at it in per year return, it is an increase of over 7% per year and if you add dividends, it has increased at a rate of over 9% per year. But achieving this growth is only possible if clients get rid of the luggage that hinders them from reaching a comfortable retirement.

Below is a summary of solutions to the largest pieces of luggage being carried around (slaying the hydra-headed beast):

- Money should be viewed as purchasing power, as a loaf of bread costs more today than ten years ago and will cost more ten years from now.

- You must have a financial plan that can grow your money as the cost of living continues to grow. The prior practice of the average couple moving into retirement was to shift a large portion of their portfolio to bonds for both income production and less volatility, but that just doesn't work. Once the average couple understands money as purchasing power and life expectancies continue to rise, the wisdom begins.

- Your behavior may be your greatest obstacle to achieving the retirement and wealth you seek. Understanding the principles of behavioral investing and how your behavior may impact your financial plan is a key to growing your wealth. Investor behavior is not simply buying and selling at the wrong time; it is the psychological traps, events, and misconceptions that cause investors to act irrationally.

- The principles are imperative to the success of investors' lifetime achievement to true multigenerational wealth. Why? They represent the belief system that directs decision making. And as we are all aware, what you think dictates what you do. Said another way, belief leads to actions.

    - Mindset is your belief or lack of belief in the future.
    - Patience means remaining calm when all others are not and allowing the process to work, even though it seems to be taking forever.
    - Discipline is the act of not *reacting* by doing what has always worked.

- The practices of Asset Allocation, Diversification, and Rebalancing become a natural progression, which can manifest into an investor's long-term, real-life returns required to provide dignity and independence in a potential three-decade retirement.

- There is a structured, financial planning process that contains seven steps and has been developed by Certified Financial Planning Board Code of Ethics and Standards of Conduct, and a CERTIFIED FINANCIAL PLANNER™ must act as a fiduciary. Picking investments, buying low, and selling high do not a plan make.

- The next end of the world crisis—like the last end of the world crisis—is not the end of the world. It just seems like it when you're in the midst of the storm.

- A financial plan or financial planning is essentially an act of delayed gratification, setting aside today's dollars to achieve a stated goal for you, your family, or multiple generations of family in the future.

- The reality of market corrections is this: since 1980 the market has dropped on average 13.8% per year. Again, the key words are *per year*. In most years, there has also been a rise that more than overcomes the drop. However, despite the temporary dips each and every year, the market has been positive 30 of those 40 years or 75% of the time.

- The value to working with a financial planner has been quantified by multiple studies, particularly when the advisor acts as a behavioral coach. The benefit (although not shown on our monthly investment statement) is reaped by not making the big emotional mistakes and instead following the plan and stewardship of the one you have entrusted with your family's multigenerational wealth.

I began this book with two points I asked you to read, pause, and read again. I would like to reiterate the same two points for reflection:

- All successful investing is goal-focused and planning driven. In contrast, all failed investing is market-focused and event-driven.

- All successful investors act constantly on their plans. Conversely, all failed investors react continually to the markets.

And finally, this may sound familiar as it has been a theme of this book, I leave you with the following:

Planning is a disciplined process of navigating rationality while enduring the uncertainties of life's challenges.

Compliance Disclaimers

"Melone Private Wealth, LLC is a registered investment advisor. Advisory services are only offered to clients or prospective clients where Melone Private Wealth and its representatives are properly licensed or exempt from licensure.

*Award based on 10 objective criteria associated with providing quality services to clients such as credentials, experience, and assets under management among other factors. Wealth managers do not pay a fee to be considered or placed on the final list of 2019 Five Star Wealth Managers.

"The inclusion of a wealth manager on The FIVE STAR Wealth Manager Award list should not be construed as an endorsement of the wealth nor should it be inferred that the responses used from the survey represent the experience of any clients. This award does not evaluate the quality of service provided and the wealth manager may have had unfavorable ratings. The rating is not indicative of the wealth manager's future performance."

The information provided is for educational and informational purposes only and does not constitute investment advice and it should not be relied on as such. It should not be considered a solicitation to buy or an offer to sell a security. It does not take into account any investor's particular investment objectives, strategies, tax status or investment horizon. You should consult your attorney or tax advisor.

The views expressed in this commentary are subject to change based on market and other conditions. These documents may contain certain statements that may be deemed forward-looking statements. Please note that any such statements are not guarantees of any future performance and actual results or developments may differ materially from those projected. Any projections, market outlooks, or estimates are based upon certain assumptions and should not be construed as indicative of actual events that will occur.

The CERTIFIED FINANCIAL PLANNER™, CFP® and federally registered CFP® (with flame design) marks (collectively, the "CFP® marks") are professional certification marks granted in the United States by Certified Financial Planner Board of Standards, Inc. ("CFP® Board"). The CFP® certification is a voluntary certification; no federal or state law or regulation requires financial planners to hold CFP® certification. It is recognized in the United States and a number of other countries for its (1) high standard of professional education; (2) stringent code of conduct and standards of practice; and (3) ethical requirements that govern professional engagements with clients. Currently, more than 71,000 individuals have obtained CFP® certification in the United States.

To attain the right to use the CFP® marks, an individual must satisfactorily fulfill the following requirements:

Education – Complete an advanced college-level course of study addressing the financial planning subject areas that CFP® Board's studies have determined as necessary for the competent and professional delivery of financial planning services and attain a bachelor's degree from a regionally accredited United States college or university (or its equivalent from a foreign university). CFP® Board's financial planning subject areas include insurance planning and risk management, employee benefits planning, investment planning, income tax planning, retirement planning, and estate planning.

Examination – Pass the comprehensive CFP® Certification Examination. The examination includes case studies and client scenarios designed to test one's ability to correctly diagnose financial planning issues and apply one's knowledge of financial planning to real world circumstances; Experience – Complete at least three years of full-time financial planning-related experience (or the equivalent, measured as 2,000 hours per year); and Ethics – Agree to be bound by CFP® Board's Standards of Professional Conduct, a set of documents outlining the ethical and practice standards for CFP® professionals.

Individuals who become certified must complete the following ongoing education and ethics requirements in order to maintain the right to continue to use the CFP® marks: Continuing Education – Complete 30 hours of continuing education hours every two years, including two hours on the Code of Ethics and other parts of the Standards of Professional Conduct, to maintain competence and keep up with developments in the financial planning field; and

Ethics – Renew an agreement to be bound by the Standards of Professional Conduct. The Standards prominently require that CFP® professionals provide financial planning services at a fiduciary standard of care. This means CFP® professionals must provide financial planning services in the best interests of their clients.

CFP® professionals who fail to comply with the above standards and requirements may be subject to CFP® Board's enforcement process, which could result in suspension or permanent revocation of their CFP® certification.

Market data was sourced using: Russell Investments July 2020, Advice Study Vanguard Advisor Alpha March 2014, Financial Planning Study KITCES April 2019 article.

As of date published, Securities offered through LPL Financial, Member FINRA/SIPC

IMPORTANT INFORMATION AND DISCLOSURES

Please remember that all investments carry some level of risk, including the potential loss of principal invested. They do not typically grow at an even rate of return and may experience negative growth. As with any type of portfolio structuring, attempting to reduce risk and increase return could, at certain times, unintentionally reduce returns.

Diversification and strategic asset allocation do not assure profit or protect against loss in declining markets.

The Investment Company Institute is the national trade association of U.S. investment companies, which includes mutual funds, closed-end funds, exchange-traded funds and unit investment trusts.

Bloomberg Barclays U.S. Aggregate Bond Index: An index, with income reinvested, generally representative of intermediate term government bonds, investment grade corporate debt securities, and mortgage-backed securities (specifically: Barclays Government/ Corporate Bond Index, the Asset – Backed Securities Index, and the Mortgage-Backed Securities Index).

FTSE EPRA/NAREIT Developed Index: A global market capitalization weighted index composed of listed real estate securities in the North American, European, and Asian real estate markets.

MSCI Emerging Markets Index: A float-adjusted market capitalization index that consists of indices in 21 emerging economies: Brazil, Chile, China, Colombia, Czech Republic, Egypt, Hungary, India, Indonesia, Korea, Malaysia, Mexico, Morocco, Peru, Philippines, Poland, Russia, South Africa, Taiwan, Thailand, and Turkey.

The MSCI EAFE Index is an equity index which captures large – and mid-cap representation across 21 developed markets countries around the world, excluding the U.S. and Canada. With 918 constituents, the index covers approximately 85% of the free float-adjusted market capitalization in each country. Countries include: Australia, Austria, Belgium, Denmark, Finland, France, Germany, Hong Kong, Ireland, Israel, Italy, Japan, the Netherlands, New Zealand, Norway, Portugal, Singapore, Spain, Sweden, Switzerland and the U.K.

The MSCI World ex U.S. Index tracks global stock market performance that includes developed and emerging markets but excludes the U.S.

The Russell 1000® Index measures the performance of the large-cap segment of the U.S. equity universe. It is a subset of the Russell 3000® Index and includes approximately 1,000 of the largest securities based on a combination of their market cap and current index membership.

The Russell 1000® Growth Index measures the performance of the large-cap growth segment of the U.S. equity universe. It includes those Russell 1000 companies with higher price-to-book ratios and higher forecasted growth values.

The Russell 1000® Value Index measures the performance of the large-cap value segment of the U.S. equity universe. It includes those Russell 1000 companies with lower price-to-book ratios and lower expected growth values.

The Russell 2000® Index measures the performance of the small-cap segment of the U.S. equity universe. The Russell 2000 Index is a subset of the Russell 3000® Index representing approximately 10% of the total market capitalization of that index. It includes approximately 2,000 of the smallest securities based on a combination of their market cap and current index membership.

The Russell 3000® Index measures the performance of the largest 3,000 U.S. companies representing approximately 98% of the investable U.S. equity market.

Indexes are unmanaged and cannot be invested in directly. Returns represent past performance, are not a guarantee of future performance, and are not indicative of any specific investment.

Past performance does not guarantee future performance.

Nothing contained in this material is intended to constitute legal, tax, securities, or investment advice, nor an opinion regarding the appropriateness of any investment, nor a solicitation of any type. The general information contained in this publication should not be acted upon without obtaining specific legal, tax, and investment advice from a licensed professional.

All Sourced Annuity Data from the site of Fisher Investments >Knowledge Center > Annuities:

- Insured Retirement Institute, 2016 IRI Fact Book (Washington, DC: IRI, 2016), 114.
- Investment Company Institute, 2017 ICI Fact Book, https://www.ici.org/pdf/2017_factbook.pdf, 89.
- Insured Retirement Institute, 2016 IRI Fact Book (Washington, DC: IRI, 2016), 102.
- Source: Insured Retirement Institute, 2011 IRI Fact Book (Washington, DC: IRI, 2011), 36-38, 56.
- Source: Securities and Exchange Commission, Variable Annuities: What You Should Know, https://www.sec.gov/reportspubs/investor-publications/investorpubsvarannty htm.html